Anthropology and Race

EUGENIA SHANKLIN

Trenton State College

Wadsworth Publishing Company
Belmont, California
A Division of Wadsworth, Inc.

Anthropology Editor: Serina Beauparlant
Editorial Assistant: Susan Shook
Production Editor: Carol Carreon Lombardi
Cover and Interior Designer: Andrew H. Ogus
Print Buyer: Diana Spence
Permissions Editor: Peggy Meehan
Copy Editor: Jan McDearmon
Signing Representative: Jeff Wilhelms
Compositor: Joan Olson
Printer: Malloy Lithographing, Inc.

Excerpts from Allan Chase, *The Legacy of Malthus.* Copyright © 1975, 1976 by Allan Chase. Reprinted by permission of Alfred A. Knopf, Inc.

Back cover photograph reprinted courtesy of Alvin H. Schulman.

*This book is printed on
acid-free recycled paper.*

International Thomson Publishing
The trademark ITP is used under license.

Printed in the United States of America.

2 3 4 5 6 7 8 9 10 — 98 97 96 95 94

Library of Congress Cataloging-in-Publication Data

Shanklin, Eugenia
    Anthropology and race / Eugenia Shanklin.
      p.   cm.
    Includes bibliographical references and index.
    ISBN 0-534-19218-1 (acid-free paper)
    1. Race. 2. Racism. 3. Anthropology—History. I. Title.
GN269.S43   1994
306—dc20   93–34316

Contents

Preface

Anthropology and Race can be used in any class that examines human evolution, culture, or genetics, or in any discussion of differences among human beings. The book's premise—that the concept of race is long overdue for an evaluation of its validity, its uses, and its abuses—will add new perspectives to introductory anthropology or sociology courses.

This book has its origins in a conversation about multicultural education that took place at a meeting of our joint sociology and anthropology department. We were reviewing our course offerings, and I asked why anthropology definitions and discussions of race were not included in a sociology course on minorities. I was told that the anthropological view was "too complicated." My first response was astonishment; my second was to look closely at what sociologists thought anthropological definitions were; my third was to write this book about anthropological explanations of differences between people, especially those differences that are called "racial." *Anthropology and Race* shows that anthropological definitions and discussions are far from being "too complicated"; they are crucial to understanding what has happened to the idea of race in the last few centuries.

HISTORY OF A CONCEPT

Prior to the eighteenth century, race was an uncommon idea in Western society, but it became enormously popular in scientific circles in the nineteenth century and underwent many changes in both scientific and popular conceptions. At present, the idea of race has been discarded by most of the scientific community because as a scientific concept it did not work very well, particularly as a device for classifying other people. But it worked altogether too well as a justificatory device for persecuting and/or exterminating millions of people in this century. This book deals with the studies of race that preoccupied members of the anthropological discipline for the last hundred years or so. I have been at pains to demonstrate that, although notions of what constitutes a race have changed dramatically in the last century, racism has continued to be an important factor in Western societies. This book also deals with the various fashions in explaining human racial differences, including current denials that race exists.

THE HABIT OF CLASSIFICATION

My hope is that by putting these ideas into perspective, students will come to understand that race is not a valid scientific concept but that it is a critical construct in folk taxonomies (including those that underpin most social sciences). A folk taxonomy is the popular way of naming or classifying things, of categorizing perceived differences. Classifying and naming things is a favorite human pastime. In the second chapter of Genesis, God asks Adam to name the animals in Eden:

> So God formed out of the soil various wild beasts and birds of the sky
> and brought them to the man to see what he called them; whatever
> the man would call a living creature, that was to be its name. The
> man gave names to all cattle, all birds of the sky, and all wild
> beasts . . . (Genesis 2:19-20).

Soon after, Adam and Eve named and classified each other as well as the relatives: husband, wife, father, mother, son, daughter-in-law, and so on.

All human groups have such classifications—of relatives, of animals, of plants, of whatever is important in their world. These classifications form an important part of our understandings of the world; they are the basis of many of our judgments. We learn them early in the simplest terms by first learning opposites, such as up/down, front/back, in/out, human/animal, light/dark, good/bad, mine/yours, he/she, we/they. Probably one of the oldest classifications is between Us and Them, or our group and theirs.

One of the "universals" anthropologists find in every society is that each group's name for itself means "human" or "people," or some variant thereof, and its name for other groups means semi- or non-human. "We" are "human," others are borderline, nearly or almost human. Some anthropologists have suggested that the adaptive value of this practice is that it allows us to predict the behavior of other groups, thereby reducing the tensions and uncertainties of dealing with strangers. They believe that constructing the "Other" draws boundaries between one's own (human) group and the Other (semi-human) group, that our construction of "Those Others" as the opposite of ourselves

(They are incestuous, lazy, dirty, and so on) makes us feel good about ourselves and lets us deny our own less-good impulses, thus lending coherence or
sanctity to the "Us" part of the equation.

If all human groups construct the Other in the same way, then, why do
some—especially Western or EuroAmerican—groups add the dimension of
"race" or physical differences to the mix? Distinctions between groups have
been made on many, or indeed, almost any, grounds—religious (They worship
the Devil), ethnic (They marry their sisters), linguistic (They insist on speak-
ing Gaelic instead of English), cultural (They eat dogs), political (They aren't
smart enough to understand democracy)—without invoking physical differences. One but only one of the reasons that We—Westerners or EuroAmeri-
cans—believe that "racial" differences exist is that anthropologists helped us to
perceive physical differences between groups as significant and meaningful.

ANTHROPOLOGY'S MIXED CONTRIBUTION

If anthropology has elaborated racial thinking, however, it has also condemned
it. It is important to understand the mixed role that anthropology has had in
the elaboration of, and challenges to, racist thinking. The history of anthropology as handmaiden of colonial expansion and administration is a major
element in the construction of the discipline. At the same time, anthropology has offered the most sustained and articulated challenge to racism, particularly in science. Students who miss either of these points have not been well
served by their courses nor by their textbooks. The support of scientists for
both the definitions of race as a reality and for the social, economic, or political consequences of these definitions are disturbing aspects of the history of
science. Anthropology's record in this respect is quite mixed—at the same
time that leading anthropologists upheld the idea of race and used it to
"prove" that other groups were inferior, other leading anthropologists
denounced the idea and offered different proofs of human equality.

A NEW APPROACH

We live in a world in which it is considered impolite or "politically incor-
rect" to notice that differences exist. But we also participate in a legislative
system in which legislation based on those differences continues to be passed.
I want students to think deeply about the political realities and the effects of
racism in the United States, because they are the ones who will have the votes
and who will have to live with and correct this generation's mishandling of
issues. I also want them to be able to evaluate statements about human physical differences, not simply refer to scientific hassles about whether differences
exist or have meaning. Race was one of the primary issues of the twentieth
century; it need not and should not be one of the primary issues of the twenty-
first. The idea of race is presented here as a sociological one, not as a valid
scientific or physical description; it is considered neither a rational explanation nor a scientific basis for the study of human differences.

STRUCTURE OF THE BOOK

Chapter 1 describes the nineteenth-century elaboration of the idea of the Irish "race" and the circumstances under which that idea changed and was discarded. The logic that accompanies current changes in thinking about race and racism is also examined, through a brief survey of current American definitions of race as a bipolar concept—Whites and Others—and with examples ranging from the discovery and glorification of Piltdown Man, whose remains were considered proof positive that humans evolved first in the West, through the invention of slavery in America and the recent Mitochondrial Eve hypothesis, which suggests that all humans are descended from one African woman who lived about 200,000 years ago.

Chapter 2 surveys the study of differences and the attempts to explain how those differences came into being, from Herodotus and Empedocles, who wrote in the sixth century B.C., through to nineteenth-century formulations of evolutionary theory. That evolution was misapplied to the study of human differences had far-reaching consequences, including the implementation of racist ideas about inferior and superior humans. The chapter also covers popular ideas about how evolution works and illustrates fallacious notions with the example of okapis (ancestors of the giraffe) and giraffes.

Chapter 3 presents ideas held by Charles Darwin and by Alfred Russel Wallace, both of whom discovered the workings of natural selection, and examines their (very different) explanations of differences between themselves and the indigenous peoples they met during their travels. Darwin's and Wallace's reactions to the people they encountered are interesting in and of themselves, but looking closely at the two men and their attempts to incorporate their reactions into their science gives us new insights into the changes in thinking about racial and cultural differences over the last century. Darwin's views are now considered somewhat old-fashioned and something of an embarrassment; Wallace's could be taken as the basis for modern or post-modern thinking about differences. Neither man's work should be taken as a model for the understanding of other cultures; what is important in the contrast is that these two men were looking at essentially the same phenomena at approximately the same time and drawing very different conclusions.

Darwin's opinions were not unique in his time and, had he been just another voyager to the outer reaches of the world, his ideas would have languished in obscurity, as Wallace's have. But Darwin's opinions about slavery and his mistaken impressions of Native Americans, especially about the "savages" of Tierra del Fuego, became part of his evolutionary theories and thus have had considerable influence on scholars for more than a century.

Chapter 4 traces the uses of the idea of race in typological theory, which was incorporated into Darwinian theory to provide justifications in eugenicist thinking for sterilization, extermination, and, most of all, discrimination. This chapter also considers the various "scientific" methods used to investigate race until the 1960s and explores the work of Franz Boas, who began the anthropological critique of race as a misleading, nonuseful scientific concept and whose students carried his ideas into the 1960s, when "race" was largely discarded in anthropology. A good example of the misuse of race as a scientific concept is the dispute over the cause and cure of pellagra, which I include to help students appreciate the far-reaching impact of the eugenics movement, as it illustrates the translation of racism into public policy.

The fifth and final chapter looks once more at the ideology of racism that is current in our world and at ways in which racism is or might be studied today. Here, too, the distinctions between racism and scientific racism or biological determinism are considered, and some of the social costs of racism are delineated. I also briefly deconstruct the race concept, as it is currently understood in America, and discuss the construction of ideas about the Other, as these are currently understood by anthropologists. Finally, I make some suggestions about rethinking and reformulating concepts.

Anthropologists have abandoned the study of race as a reality and, along with it, the study of racism and scientific racism. I applaud the former decision, deplore the latter, and believe that we need to take up the study of racism again and carry it to a new level of understanding, one that will help to neutralize its potency in the minds of the generations to come.

ACKNOWLEDGMENTS

This book has many sources and has been many years in the making. My thanks, in temporal order, go to Joseph B. Birdsell, who first told me about okapis and piqued my interest in evolutionary questions; to Sidney W. Mintz and a grant from the National Endowment for the Humanities, both of which initiated the process of writing; to Trenton State College, which made helpful contributions in many forms, including released time, encouragement, and computer equipment; to Howard Robboy, Chair of the Sociology-Anthropology Department; and Richard Kamber, Dean of Arts and Sciences, who facilitated all cheerfully and, more important, quickly; and to my anthropology students over the years who have served as guinea pigs of enormously useful persuasions—Doubting Thomases, Devil's Advocates, and Popular Audience; to Robert W. Sussman, careful reader and reliable critic; to the members of the Princeton Research Forum; to my husband, Alvin H. Schulman, whose patience is nothing short of miraculous; and to the Wadsworth staff, whose enthusiasm and interest have been inspirational. I thank the following colleagues for their contributions to the development of this text: Garland E. Allen, Washington University in St. Louis; Joe Feagin, University of Florida; Lawrence Hirschfeld, University of Michigan; Richard Robbins, State University of New York, Plattsburgh; and Brackette Williams, University of Arizona. I also thank Anthony Appiah, Harvard University, and C. Loring Brace, University of Michigan, for their valuable input.

Conversations with Loring Brace, Alice Brues, Clara Rodriguez, and many others contributed to this book but the mistakes are mine alone.

●

Race as a Social Category,
Not a Biological Fact

One of my reasons for writing this book is to put together two ideas of race—as a folk (sociological) concept and as a failed and discarded analytic (biological) concept—into an intelligible, accessible whole, a work that discusses problems with the concept of race on many levels. Another reason is that I have grown weary of explaining to my students that there is no such thing as a scientific concept of race. If, as we will see, Hitler knew this in the 1930s, why are college students in the 1990s so ill-informed on the subject? This then is a book about race for cultural anthropology students, or indeed anyone interested in the social sciences. It is not a technical treatise about populations and clines and other technical terms now used by biologists to describe differences between groups. The emphasis here is on the contrast between folk conceptions of race and what scientists used to consider scientific grounds for defining human races. Banton calls these the "folk" and "analytical" uses of the term and points out that there is "a two-way traffic between the two spheres of discourse" (1987:xiv). He adds that folk concepts change through time:

> Thus people in twentieth-century Europe do not explain misfortune and mental illness in terms of the concepts of witchcraft and madness used by their ancestors. Folk concepts are also modified in line with popular experience: ideas about other peoples change in step with the frequency and character of the encounters from which that experience is derived. So

in the course of time folk concepts acquire additional meanings which increase their serviceability in everyday communication while introducing ambiguities (Banton 1987:xiii).

In America, folk concepts of race continue to draw credibility from the scientific inconclusiveness about race that so many authors are careful to mention. The distinction between the failed, discarded biological concept of race and the ongoing popular concept of race must be clearly drawn if students are to understand the fallacies of racism.

In the notes to his book, *Strangers in the Land*, John Higham muses that "To a surprising degree the history of race-thinking on both sides of the Atlantic has been neglected, perhaps partly because our sense of guilt makes detachment difficult to achieve, and partly because the subject requires a grasp of both scientific and social thought" (1981:406). Nancy Stepan echoes the sentiment: "Rather surprisingly, considering the long history of social Darwinism and racism, the racial ideas of the founding figures of evolutionism have never been examined systematically and in depth" (1982:48). I think the reason for the gaps is more convoluted than these authors suggest, but this book is an attempt to bring together several strands in understanding modern anthropological ideas about race, racism, and their effects.

Anthropological consciousness about race has changed considerably since the 1950s and 1960s, when anthropologists, following the lead of Franz Boas and his students, wrote books on the subject. Margaret Mead said that Boas encouraged all his students to participate in major debates of the day. In recent years, however, anthropologists appear to have lost that urge and with it, the inclination to participate in ongoing discussions of racism.

Popular conceptions about race have also changed in the last four or five decades. Think, for example, of the changes in the words used to describe African-Americans in the last few decades: in the 1960s, Negro was the correct phrase; then black or Afro-American became the standard; now African-American is the appropriate phrase. We have moved from a "racial" description to a color description and on to an ethnic-group designation. Perhaps, in the twenty-first century, we will be able to abandon all such designations.

From the beginnings of their disciplines, social scientists have faced the problem of explaining differences among people. One solution, popular until a few decades ago, was the idea of race; but ideas about what constitutes a race, as well as scientific definitions of the word itself, have changed dramatically in the last century. They are still changing. The emphasis of this chapter is, first, on changes in perceptions about what a race is and, second, on the uses that can be and have been made of different understandings of race. Until the mid-twentieth century, many social scientists would have said yes, if asked whether physical differences between people were indicators of other (mental) abilities. Going into the twenty-first century, most social scientists will say no. In the recent past, respected anthropologists appeared on both sides in these debates, but since the 1950s, anthropologists have all but abandoned the concept of race, as well as the belief that other characteristics, such as IQ scores, are associated with apparent physical differences. The recent virtual silence of anthropology on the subject of race, however, may have encouraged students to believe both that physical differences are real and that they have meaningful associations with other nonphysical characteristics.

But if race is not a useful scientific concept, racism—the belief that physical characteristics are inevitably associated with mental or emotional capacities—continues to be a major social problem, and the fuzziness of definitions of race does not help in solving the social ills caused by racism. Racism is a heightened form of ethnocentrism (the belief that one's own people or lifeways are better than all others). Holding racist or ethnocentric ideas is a bit like believing that the stork brings babies—many of us may start out that way, but as we get closer to adulthood we learn that the reality is far more interesting than the myth.

Anthropologists have abandoned the concept of race but not the study of how one group characterizes the differences between themselves and others; in America, physical differences, especially skin color differences, are interpreted according to a "biracial" system of differentiation—there is white and there is nonwhite. These categories are interpreted according to a vague principle of biological descent, a principle perpetuated in social science textbook discussions of race.

"WHITE NATIVES"

The following quotations concern a group of "white natives." How many people could correctly identify the group?

> This people, then, is truly barbarous, being not only barbarous in their dress, but suffering their hair and beards to grow enormously in an uncouth manner, just like the modern fashion recently introduced; indeed, all their habits are barbarisms (Wright's 1892 translation of a twelfth-century text by Giraldus Cambrensis, quoted in Curtis 1968:124).

> Wherefore this is a race of savages: I say again a race of utter savages. For not merely are they uncouth of garb, but they also let their hair and beards grow to outrageous length, something like the newfangled fashion which has lately come in with us. In short, all their ways are brutish and unseemly (Barnard's 1910 translation of the same text, quoted in Curtis 1968:124).

> But I am haunted by the human chimpanzees I saw along that hundred miles of horrible country. I don't believe they are our fault. I believe there are not only many more of them than of old, but that they are happier, better, more comfortably fed and lodged under our rule than they ever were. But to see white chimpanzees is dreadful; if they were black, one would not feel it so much, but their skins, except where tanned by exposure, are as white as ours (Kingsley 1860, quoted in Curtis 1968:84).

[They are] more like tribes of squalid apes than human beings . . . as
unstable as water . . . an impatience of control, a deliberate preference for
disorder, a determination in each individual man to go his own way,
whether it was a good way or a bad, and a reckless hatred of industry
(Froude 1845 and later, quoted in Curtis 1968:84–86).

[They are] the sons and daughters of generations of beggars. You can
trace the descent in their blighted, stunted forms—in their brassy, cun-
ning, brutalized features. [Their huts are] . . . monuments to national
idleness and they themselves are the missing link between the gorilla and
the Negro (*Punch* 1849, quoted in Lebow 1976:40).

[They] would rather gain possession by their blood than by their labour. . . .

The murders of this country would disgrace the most gloomy wilds of
the most savage tribes that ever roamed in Asia, Africa, or America.

Their very amusements are polemical: fighting is a pastime which
they seldom assemble without enjoying. . . . When not driven by neces-
sity, they willingly consume whole days in sloth, or as willingly employ
them in riot; strange diversity of nature to love indolence and hate
quiet—to be reduced to slavery, but not yet to obedience.

. . . their turbulent spirit is so averse to order and peace that no prince
or legislator their country ever produced was able to control them (early
eighteenth-century writers, quoted in Lebow 1976:46).

Did anyone guess that these "human chimpanzees" or "squalid apes"
were the Irish, as the English saw or claimed to see them? The first two
quotations are from a twelfth-century English description ordered by Henry
II, who reigned from 1154 to 1189, and planned to invade Ireland. To
sanction the invasion, Henry wanted the Pope's blessing and he obtained it
after sending Giraldus Cambrensis, a Welsh monk, to Ireland to gather the
evidence that he needed, eyewitness evidence that the Irish were heathen
and uncivilized. Disinformation campaigns are not new, though the phrase
may be.

Three hundred years before, in the ninth century, Charlemagne used Ireland for a different purpose: when he wanted his courtiers to learn to read
and write, he sent messengers to Ireland to bring back Irish monks to his
court, from which he sent them off to spread literacy throughout Europe.

The Welsh Cambrensis found no community of literate, scholarly monks,
toiling away at illuminating manuscripts; instead he obligingly described the
"wild Irish as eaters of human flesh, murderers and thieves who reveled in
sodomy and incest. Irish religion . . . consisted of pagan beliefs in a nomi-
nally Christian form that served only to guarantee the ascendancy of the bards
and uncivilized priests over the ignorant people. . . . the religion incited people to the most wanton cruelty and was primarily responsible for their
degraded character" (Cambrensis, quoted in Lebow 1976:75).

Scholars like L. P. Curtis have noted that what was for Henry II and his
supporters an imaginary and useful idea became ever more a social reality in

the minds of the English governors of Ireland (Lebow 1976:81). By the middle of the nineteenth century, Curtis adds, the idea of the degenerate Irish "race" was one of three guiding notions that provided the impetus for British domination of Ireland: the other two were class and religion. The Irish were not Anglo-Saxon, as were their conquerors; nor were they upper class and Protestant, as were their colonists. By exalting their own Saxon heritage, the English were able to believe themselves justified in what Curtis calls "their confiscatory and homicidal habits in that country" (1968:18). Lebow makes a different point: at the same time the English were dismissing the Irish as racially inferior, as unsuited to self-governance, they were embarked at home on a program of political reform, of increasing democracy, liberty, and humaneness.

Why did this happen? What was the purpose of reducing a group of people to the status of "savages" or "human chimpanzees"? What were the social effects of these denunciations? Clearly Henry II's purposes were political; he needed an excuse to invade a country and he used Cambrensis to prove that Ireland was such a degenerate place that only English domination would enable the inhabitants to become part of the human race.

But once English domination of Ireland was established, the ideas that began with Henry II in the twelfth century prevailed and spread to the community at large, with social and economic effects far beyond their original political purposes. Scientists, too, lent their authority to the notion of an Irish or Celtic race; in his influential work, *The Descent of Man*, Charles Darwin quoted with approval the "findings" of Mr. Greg:

> A most important obstacle in civilised countries to an increase in the number of men of a superior class has been strongly insisted on by Mr. Greg and Mr. Galton, namely that the poor and reckless, who are often degraded by vice, almost invariably marry early, whilst the careful and frugal, who are generally otherwise virtuous, marry late in life. . . .
>
>   . . . as Mr. Greg puts the case: "The careless, squalid, unaspiring Irishman multiplies like rabbits: the frugal, foreseeing, self-respecting, ambitious Scot, . . . passes his best years in struggle and in celibacy, marries late, and leaves few behind him. Given a land originally peopled by a thousand Saxons and a thousand Celts—and in a dozen generations five-sixths of the population would be Celts, but five-sixths of the property, of the power, of the intellect, would belong to the one-sixth of Saxons that remained. In the eternal 'struggle for existence,' it would be the inferior and *less* favoured race that had prevailed—and prevailed by virtue not of its good qualities but of its faults" (Darwin 1898:140–141).

Notions about the "degenerate" Irish race were carried to America, especially as the Irish immigrated in huge numbers after the Potato Famine of the 1850s. One place in which the Irish "race" idea became popular was New England, particularly in Boston, where large groups of Irish settled. The history of relations between the Brahmins, as the ruling group of Boston was called, and the Irish immigrants has been discussed eloquently and often by historians such as Oscar Handlin (1951, 1954), Edward N. Saveth (1948), and Barbara M. Solomon (1956). At first, the Brahmins discounted notions of race in trying to account for what they saw as aberrant Irish behavior (Solomon 1956:116). The Irish immigrants disturbed the Boston Brahmins for different reasons than they had the English. The Irish were fiercely Anglophobic, whereas the Brahmins were Anglophiles; the Irish became Democrats and voted in blocs for people who believed in political patronage, whereas the Brahmins were Republicans and believers in the democratic process; the Irish entered enthusiastically into labor movements, including violent ones such as the Molly Maguires, whereas the Brahmins often owned the companies against which the labor uprisings were directed.

Racial epithets soon appeared in the literature. James Russell Lowell, an influential Brahmin who, early on, denied a racial basis for Irish-American behavior, began to give credence to the idea by 1888 (Solomon 1956:55). Others followed suit, including John Fiske, the popularizer of the Anglo-Saxon legend that traced the birth of democratic ideals back to Germany and held that the English were among the principal champions of these ideals. From 1876, Hermann Eduard Von Holst wrote about the political history of the United States and opposed the Irish because he believed they were in the lowest stage of culture and exhibited inherent tendencies to violence (Saveth 1948:153). James Ford Rhodes, an influential historian whose nine-volume work appeared between 1894 and 1906, delighted in damning the Irish-Americans because of their (inherited) tendencies toward violence and intemperance (Saveth 1948:172).

By 1910, there were 1,300,000 Irish-born in the country (Handlin 1954:76), and a full-scale American nativist movement, which attempted to block further immigration that might dilute Anglo-Saxon stock, had emerged, failed, and re-emerged several times. John Higham refers these ups and downs of American nativist movements to swings in American confidence (Higham 1981), and notes that the rhetorical swings between optimistic American thinking about race—America as the great melting pot, hybrids more hardy than purebreds—and pessimism about America's future were accompanied by fulminations on the importance of racial purity or descriptions of the horrors of racial suicide (Higham 1981:152).

In 1955, an extensive study of the Irish was carried out by a team of physical anthropologists from Harvard University, led by Earnest Hooton. Although not entirely unbiased in its findings, the study made clear that there was no such thing as a distinctive Irish or Celtic race; instead there had been considerable mixture of "racial" types over centuries.

> It soon became apparent that in no part of Ireland were there any great concentrations of physical types which were peculiar to certain localities and which did not occur in other areas. In short, the population appeared to be composed of several different elements which had become thoroughly mixed over many centuries (Hooton and Dupertuis 1955:4).

There was, however, an identifiable Keltic "type":

> The term "Keltic" was applied to long heads with a combination of
> blue eyes and darkish hair or red hair. There is perhaps no set and con-
> ventional designation for this combination, but it is so common in those
> parts of Northwestern Europe where Keltic languages are spoken that
> it seemed a fairly appropriate name. As will be seen in later discussions,
> it turns out to be a linguistic misnomer. However, the physical
> type thus crudely defined is a reality and nothing hypothetical (Hooton
> and Dupertuis 1955:141).

This study seems never to have been especially influential, perhaps
because it came well after the death knell of Irish racial studies had sounded.
Historians believe the idea of an Irish race became unpopular in America once
it was clear to politicians that the Irish held positions of leadership in many
labor unions and wielded considerable political power (Handlin 1954:93). In
1969, however, one defender of the old-fashioned way of construing Irish-
English differences wrote:

> This quarrel can be understood only in terms of the profound racial dif-
> ferences between the Gaelic-speaking natives and the English-speaking
> invaders, a difference which even today, after twenty generations of lim-
> ited hybridization, is still not seriously blurred.
>   The English were sober, industrious, mechanical, calculating and
> ruthless; characteristics invaluable in government. The native Irish by
> contrast were imaginative, unpredictable and even irresponsible. Their
> pre-Aryan and perhaps paleolithic speech had died out only in the ninth
> century and they had more left of their Paleolithic instincts (Darlington
> 1969:449–450).

Most people today would never think of claiming that the Irish were a
separate race; Irish and Irish-Americans are usually included in the group
called "whites" without further discussion. What then is to be learned from
reviewing these notions about a "degenerate" or semihuman Irish race?

First, this particular example shows how much beliefs about what constitutes a "race" have changed, even in the last century.

Second, although the original purpose of creating an Irish race may have
been political, the reality of this "race" seems to have continued as a result
of political, economic, and social conditions in those countries infected by
the idea.

Third, and perhaps most puzzling, is that freedom and equality were
increasing in England at the same time that those rights were being denied
to the Irish. Nor was this a unique phenomenon: something similar happened
in seventeenth-century colonial Virginia, where slavery, in its American sense,
was invented and the rights of Africans were taken away. Edmund Morgan
calls this "rise of liberty and equality . . . accompanied by the rise of slavery" the "central paradox of American history" (1972:5-6).

SLAVERY IN AMERICA

Africans were brought to the colonies as slaves but once there, they "enjoyed the same rights and duties as other Virginians" (Morgan 1972:17) and, until the last quarter of the seventeenth century, were subject to the same laws. Africans could buy their own freedom, own land, cattle, and houses, and sue or be sued in court. But by 1676, there was a new and dangerous group of freedmen in Virginia, men who had come as servants, served their terms, and on their release from service could not find work or land. They were armed, as Virginians had to be at that time, and discontented. Morgan says:

> To be sure, the men at the bottom might have had both land and liberty, as the settlers of some other colonies did, if Virginia's frontier had been safe from Indians, or if the men at the top had been willing to forego some of their profits and to give up some of the lands they had engrossed. The English government itself made efforts to break up the great holdings that had helped to create the problem. But it is unlikely that the policy makers in Whitehall would have contended long against the successful.
>
> In any case they did not have to. There was another solution, which allowed Virginia's magnates to keep their lands, yet arrested the discontent and the repression of other Englishmen, a solution which strengthened the rights of Englishmen and nourished that attachment to liberty which came to fruition in the Revolutionary generation of Virginia statesmen.
>
> . . . The rights of Englishmen were preserved by destroying the rights of Africans (1972:24).

Morgan agrees with Winthrop Jordan (1968) that this was not a deliberate move and that slavery probably came to Virginia as an unthinking decision, an automatic result when Virginians bought the cheapest labor they could get. The courts moved to restrict the rights of "Negroes," and by 1690, "slavery began to assume its now familiar character as a complete deprivation of all rights" (Jordan 1968:82). Separate laws were made to govern Negroes and whites. By this means, the problem of the roving freedmen was solved:

> Nor is it surprising that Virginia's freedmen never again posed a threat to society. Though in later years slavery was condemned because it was thought to compete with free labor, in the beginning it reduced by so much the number of freedmen who would otherwise have competed with each other. When the annual increment of freedmen fell off, the number that remained could more easily find an independent place in society. . . . There might still remain a number of irredeemable, idle, and unruly freedmen, particularly among the convicts whom England exported to the colonies. But the numbers were small enough, so that they could be dealt with by the old expedient of drafting them for military expeditions. The way was thus made easier for the remaining freedmen to acquire property, maybe acquire a slave or two of their own, and

join with their superiors in the enjoyment of those English liberties that differentiated them from their black laborers (Morgan 1972:27–28).

Jordan points out that slavery did not cause prejudice, nor did prejudice cause slavery. Instead the two "generated each other" (1968:80). But this was not the only result of America's central paradox:

It was slavery . . . more than any other single factor, that had made the difference, slavery that enabled Virginia to nourish representative government in a plantation society, slavery that transformed the Virginia of Governor Berkeley to the Virginia of Jefferson, slavery that made the Virginians dare to speak a political language that magnified the rights of freemen, and slavery, therefore, that brought Virginians into the same commonwealth political tradition with New Englanders. . . . Thus began the American paradox of slavery and freedom, intertwined and interdependent, the rights of Englishmen supported on the wrongs of Africans . . . (Morgan 1972:289).

Scholars have long debated the question of the concomitant rise of freedom and of various forms of repression (racism, slavery, colonial domination), and the suggested explanations are sometimes more thought-provoking than conclusive. Orlando Patterson (1991) has suggested that our Western notion of freedom was generated from the experience of slavery. To extrapolate Patterson's sophisticated and well-documented argument, we might say that freedom and repression are social qualities maintained in internal and/or external balance, that freedom for some members of a society (or an entire society) increases at the expense of other members of the society (or another society).

A second explanation is that freedom is a function or result of the accessibility of resources; for example, the British invasion of other countries was a result of economic imperatives to do with expanding mercantile capitalism, and freedom at home (in England) was a result of greater resource accessibility abroad (in Ireland).

Whatever the accepted explanation, the correlation between increases in both repressions and freedoms is well documented in the scholarly literature and with it, the use of political propaganda to convince people that those "others" (whose rights are being taken away) thoroughly deserve their fate.

Should anyone doubt that political expedience underlies invocations or conceptions of race and racial differences, we can take other examples, from the twentieth century. Richard Milner writes about the Yanomamo of Brazil, studied by Napoleon Chagnon (a case familiar to anthropologists and anthropology students), that in 1989 Chagnon's writings "were being used by the Brazilian government to argue that these tribesmen are murderous, primitive people, incapable of being absorbed into the life of a modern nation. Not so coincidentally, gold has been discovered in their province, and 'sociobiological' arguments about their hereditary fierceness gives a convenient 'scientific' excuse for treating them as less than human" (1990:380).

Another example comes from the words of a well-known twentieth-century leader, who discussed the problems with the idea of nationhood and suggested they might be overcome by substituting the concept of race:

> The conception of the nation has become meaningless . . . "the nation" is a political expedient of democracy and liberalism. We have to . . . set in its place the conception of race. . . . The new order cannot be conceived in terms of the national boundaries of the peoples of the historic past, but in terms of race that transcends those boundaries. . . . *I know perfectly well . . . that in a scientific sense there is no such thing as race* . . . but I as a politician need a conception which enables the order which has hitherto existed on historic bases to be abolished and an entirely new and antihistoric order enforced and given an intellectual basis. . . . And for this purpose the conception of races serves me well. . . . With the conception of race, National Socialism will carry its revolution abroad and recast the world [emphasis added].

These are the words of Adolf Hitler (quoted in Rauschning 1940: 231–232), who tried to do what he promised: to use the idea of race, which he knew to be an unscientific concept, to rebuild Germany, not on historical but on racial grounds.

These examples illustrate another point as well: Scientists are not immune to the prejudices and ideas currently in vogue. If as eminent a scientist as Charles Darwin could endorse the notion of a Celtic race, it is not surprising that Earnest Hooton saw a Keltic physical type. As Anaïs Nin put it, "We don't see things as they are; we see things as we are."

The creation of the Irish "race" is one way in which scientists illustrated both their human fallibility and their ethnocentrism, that is, their belief that their own culture was the "right" or best one, that all other cultures were inferior.[1] Another example of scientists seeing what they wanted to see may be found in the reaction to the Piltdown forgery. Soon after the details of the Irish race had been worked out, a new fossil find came to light in England and for forty years dominated the thinking of most scientists concerned with human evolution.

THE PILTDOWN FORGERY

Darwin's oracular pronouncement at the conclusion of *The Origin of Species,* "Much light will be thrown on the origins of man and his history," was expanded in *The Descent of Man,* where Darwin noted his belief that fossil evidence for human evolution would surface—probably, Darwin speculated, in the tropics and possibly in Africa, where two of our closest living relatives, the chimpanzee and the gorilla, were found. European finds, particularly those from the Neander Valley, were the subject of hot disputes in Darwin's lifetime, some believing that the fossils were those of deformed individuals and that there was no such thing as fossil "man" (Cuvier, quoted in Eldredge and

Tattersall 1982:67–68), and others believing that the newly found skeletal material represented a link with early humans (Keith and others). Into this fray came Piltdown Man or *Eoanthropus*, "Dawn Man," proof that the earliest hominids lived in England.

In 1912, Arthur Smith Woodward announced the find: parts of a skull belonging to a large-brained hominid had been found in the Piltdown gravels of Sussex. By 1913, the bits had been assembled and they included the back and left side of a skull, the right rear portion of a jaw, and a single tooth. Piltdown Man was taken as proof that the first large-brained human ancestor had evolved in England. Sir Arthur Keith, a leading anatomist of the time, proclaimed that the Piltdown find was "the most important ever made in England, and of equal, if not of greater importance than any other yet made, either at home or abroad" (Keith, quoted in Dawson and Woodward 1913:148).

The *Manchester Guardian* announced that

> There seems to be no doubt whatever of its genuineness, and more than a possibility of its being the oldest remnant of a human frame yet discovered on this planet. We shall probably have to wait a little while longer before the full details of the discovery and the considered verdict upon it of our highest geological and anthropological authorities are formally laid before the scientific world, but enough is already known to warrant the announcement which we make today. . . . It will be extremely interesting to learn how far it bridges the gap between the skulls of the most man-like ape and the most ape-like man so far known to science, but the fact that it has been unhesitatingly recognised as human and not simian would appear to indicate that more than half of the difference must still remain (Spencer 1990:47, quoting the *Manchester Guardian* of 21 November 1912).

Unfortunately, as Eldredge and Tattersall observe, Piltdown Man quickly became the standard against which other skeletal evidence was judged (1982:79) and, usually, found wanting. Along with many other fossil finds, Eugene Dubois's finds from Indonesia and Raymond Dart's evidence from South Africa were dismissed by a majority of the scientific community because they did not resemble Piltdown, did not show the continuities that might be expected with an upright-walking, big-brained English ancestor.

Forty years after its discovery, Piltdown Man was finally proved to be a fake, an ingenious combination of a modern human skull and an ape jawbone. Since the Piltdown fragments were discredited by an analysis of their fluorine content, there has been speculation about who planted the remains. Nearly all the major figures of the scientific community, whether they were involved in the discovery, working in the vicinity, or engaged in the evaluation of the meaning of Piltdown, have been nominated as culprit: Sir Arthur Keith, the anatomist who first commented on the remains (Spencer 1990b); Charles Dawson, the amateur archaeologist who uncovered them (Weiner

1955); William Ruskin Butterfield, a museum curator with a grudge against Dawson (Spencer 1990b); Teilhard de Chardin, Jesuit priest and French paleontologist whose motives were said to be a mixture of nationalistic spite and the wish to test the gullibility of the scientific establishment (Gould 1980a); and even Sir Arthur Conan Doyle, creator of Sherlock Holmes, friend of Dawson, and dabbler in both scientific and spiritualist endeavors (Winslow and Meyer 1983). Frank Spencer reviews the evidence against all these and more before choosing Sir Arthur Keith as his particular candidate for perpetrator (1990b), whereas Lord S. Zuckerman points to Martin Hinton as the culprit (Zuckerman 1990:16). Hinton had motive, means, and opportunity, in the mystery writers' mandate: his motive was his dislike of Smith Woodward, his means was his expertise in the Pliocene fauna of the region, and his opportunity was time spent exploring the gravels in the vicinity of Piltdown. Whoever planted the Piltdown fragments saw what probably began as a joke directed against the scientific community develop quickly into an established "fact," one that brooked no dispute.

For our purposes, the question of why Piltdown Man was taken so seriously is more interesting than the identity of the perpetrator. Piltdown's treatment bears on the issue of race and racial thinking in anthropology because it illustrates the willingness of scientists to be misled by their own preconceptions, ethnocentric preconceptions in this instance, and their determination to ignore evidence not in accord with these preconceptions. It appears that many scientists wanted to see evidence of human evolution occurring first in Europe and, whatever its anomalies, Piltdown provided that evidence.

The example of the invention of the American form of slavery (and the social and economic effects underscored by racial prejudice with which contemporary Americans are still coping) illustrates some of the ways in which social and economic effects continue long after they are officially denied or denounced by politicians and scientists. Notions of what constitutes a race are still changing, and it is important to understand how those ideas have changed in anthropology and what the effects of the changes have been.

Two aspects of prejudice or bigotry have been studied for years by scholars: first, the psychological underpinnings that cause individuals to adopt or embrace these notions. A good deal of the psychological literature concerns itself with just that problem. As Curtis puts it, race is a lightning conductor, through which many emotions can be effectively discharged (Curtis 1968:20). The second aspect of the study of prejudice is its sociological causation, and this book is concerned with those sociological concepts that explain the rise and fall of stereotypical notions about human groups; that is, what we mean when we define someone as part of the "other" has to do with who and where we are, not necessarily with who and what they are. Thus the mid-Victorian era had its thinkers who believed in the inferiority of the Irish "race," and in describing the Irish used such stereotypical adjectives as "childish, emotionally unstable, ignorant, indolent, superstitious, primitive or semi-civilized, dirty, vengeful, and violent" (Curtis 1968:53). Today we have thinkers who believe in the inferiority of the Negro or black or African-American "race" and who use many of the same adjectives to describe African-Americans, as well as seemingly scientific methods to produce results that support their prejudices.

Anthropologists now understand race as a social category, not as a biological fact, although most of the writing about race as a social, not biological, category was done in the 1960s and 1970s, not the 1980s or 1990s. Claude Lévi-Strauss observed: "We discover that race—or what is generally understood by this term—is one of the functions of culture" (Lévi-Strauss 1971:657–658). In 1978, Morton Fried also defined race as an idea built into the culture's notions about how the world is divided, but he went further and noted that "race" expresses a certain kind of unresolved social conflict that thrives on divisions and invidious distinctions (1978:315).

A sample from the 1980s:

> Just as the scientific racial classifications of the 18th and 19th centuries interfaced with the racial folk classifications of the day, so racial classification today also serves a purpose in the larger social context. Unfortunately, modern scientific classification of humanity may offer reinforcement for folk taxonomies of races which have been roundly attacked on legal and moral grounds. In those cultures where caste and class systems have effectively trapped peoples of color in the lowest niches of the socioeconomic structure, scientific racial classifications frequently leave the arena of science and find varied uses in the political sphere (Collins et al. 1981:14).

In the late 1980s, Michael Banton wrote:

> "Race" is often used as if it were an objective, scientific, and culture-free designation of differences of appearance. It is not. The very use of this word to identify such a kind of classification brings with it a host of cultural associations deriving from the historical circumstances in which the word acquired a special meaning (1988:9).

If race in the 1990s is a discarded biological concept, racism is alive and well. In the late 1960s, Pierre Van den Berghe gave an excellent definition of racism:

> Racism is any set of beliefs that organic, genetically transmitted differences (whether real or imagined) between human groups are intrinsically associated with the presence or the absence of certain socially relevant abilities or characteristics, hence that such differences are a legitimate basis of invidious distinctions between groups socially defined as races (1967:11).

In the 1970s, Hunter and Whitten defined racism as

> the doctrine that the cultural and intellectual characteristics of a population are linked to its biological racial character, especially the notion that

some races are inherently superior to others. The term also denotes a social system in which certain ethnic groups are especially oppressed and exploited with the rationalization that they are racially (biologically) inferior (Hunter and Whitten 1976:328).

The same authors also point to the ebb and flow of racist thinking in America:

Students of racism in the United States have remarked that its strength appears to wax and wane with fluctuations in national economic circumstances and policies. Thus the resurgence of racist ideology at the end of the Reconstruction Era after the Civil War coincided with the decision by northern capitalists to abandon social reform in the South and reestablish their antebellum alliance with the plantation owners (1976:328).

In the 1990s, one anthropologist noted that "In describing their fellow humans, however, scientists have historically propounded the most bizarre theories, based mainly on perceived differences in culture, social traditions and their own ideas of beauty, which they, more often than not, have confused with biology" (Milner 1990:379). Milner added,

Over the past half-century, the idea of traditional "races of man" has completely broken down in science. Recent genetic studies have shown that there is more variation WITHIN geographic populations than there is between them. . . .

Racism (theories about the "natural" superiority and inferiority of human populations) carried to its limit usually leads to some group of people being systematically robbed of their land, labor, property—or exterminated altogether. Earlier in history, it was enough that they were of a different culture, religion or skin color for them to be branded animals, heathens, savages or infidels. But since science has won increasing acceptance as a source of truth, its "authority" has been cited to justify exterminations of Tasmanians and Australian aborigines by the British, Native Americans by "anglos," Jews and gypsies by Germans, and Africans by British, French, and Belgians (1990:380).

This book deals with the history of anthropological studies of human "racial" differences, with racism, and with the current anthropological understanding of race as a social classification, emphasizing the contemporary social understanding of race as a synonym for skin color, or better (in the American case), race as skin color different from "ours." Martin Marger points to a useful analogy given by Robert Redfield: "If people took special notice of red automobiles, and believed that the redness of automobiles was connected inseparably with their mechanical effectiveness, then red automobiles would constitute a real and important category" (Redfield, quoted in Marger 1994:25).

Most of what is said here is neither new nor original, but even though these ideas are commonplace in anthropology, they have not yet become part of the popular conception of race in today's world. Fried asked: "Why is it so hard to give up this miserable little four-letter word that of all four-letter words has done the most damage? Most laymen of my acquaintance, whether tolerant or bigoted, are frankly puzzled when they are told that race is an idea. It seems to them that it is something very real that they experience every day" (1978:313). Earlier, Fried called for an end to "pseudoscientific investigations of race," noting that

> Participation in a debate over racial differences in intelligence, ability, or achievement potential is not a means of asserting and spreading knowledge of the views of professionally concerned scientists. Quite the opposite, it is a means of lifting in the public eye the status of studies that are otherwise disqualified and rejected by science. . . . There is even more need to end practices whereby such studies are treated as serious intellectual endeavors. . . . [we must] recognize them for what they are, expressions of bias and propaganda tracts favoring certain social arrangements . . . (1968:129).

Many anthropologists view the search for biological certainty about race as an erroneous episode in the attempt to understand biological differences, whereas others view it as irrelevant to the study of social processes. Whatever the view, anthropologists seldom discuss "race" nowadays and when they do, it is mentioned only in passing and in heavy quotes. The anthropological norm of the 1990s was prefigured in a distinguished lecture delivered at the American Ethnological Society in 1988, when Stanley J. Tambiah, a leading anthropologist, pointed out that ethnicity, which is becoming the "master" principle of classification, is projected on old bases of identity such as language, race, religion, or place of origin (1989:336). A recent meeting of the American Anthropological Association addressed the issue of race and race differences, and the outcome, still largely unpublished (but see Alice Brues mimeo., 1991, 1992), may be that more attention will be paid in the future to these issues.

It was not always the case that anthropologists dealt summarily with the concept of race; from the mid-nineteenth century until the 1940s and 1950s, the study of human races preoccupied scientists, and many ideas were put forth that we now see as erroneous, biased, or bigoted. In the 1960s, the notion of race as a valid physical or biological category was denounced by leading anthropologists and, by about 1975, discussions of race had disappeared from most anthropology textbooks. This silence has enhanced confusion about a concept that remains current in the popular imagination, one often used to justify social and legal decisions as if its scientific basis were fully established.

Anthropologists may have thought that the reasons for their denunciations were sufficiently compelling to cause the idea of race to disappear from the social science literature. But this has not happened. A vacuum was left when anthropologists withdrew from the debates over the nature of race; into that vacuum other social scientists have put their most evocative flights of fancy. Some imagine that the scientific definitions of race were sufficiently established by 1950 and offer further embroideries on outmoded ideas. Others conjecture that the physical basis of race is still being explored, albeit with dubious results, and suggest lines for further exploration.

For example, in the fourth edition of his influential text, *Racial and Ethnic Groups*, Richard Schaefer says, "*Race* has many meanings for many people. Probably the only thing about race that is clear is that we are confused about the origins and proper use of the term" (1990:12). Schaefer then gives a precise meaning of biological race as "a genetically isolated group characterized by a high degree of inbreeding that leads to distinctive gene frequencies" (1990:12), and points to three major areas of confusion in using the term: first, disagreements about the number and characteristics of human races; second, the presence or absence of pure races and their origin; and third, the relationship of race to personality traits, such as intelligence (1990:12). Schaefer uses anthropological definitions from the 1950s and 1960s (Montagu 1964; Coon, Garn, and Birdsell 1950) to support the idea that there are somewhere between three major races and two hundred microraces but affirms that there are no mutually exclusive races (1990:12). He uses studies (Boyd 1963) from the 1960s to denounce the idea of the purity of races. The third area, the relationship of race to intelligence, he dismisses by characterizing Jensen's use of IQ testing as "unscientific."

Another popular text, Martin Marger's (1994) *Race and Ethnic Relations*, distinguishes between the biological and social meanings of race and adds that

> The essential biological meaning of *race* is a population of humans classified on the basis of certain hereditary characteristics that differentiate them from other human groups. Races are, in a sense, pigeonholes for categorizing human physical types (1994:19).

Marger goes on to add that "Whether the idea of race is meaningful in a biological sense remains a controversial and seemingly unresolvable issue. But whatever its biological validity, the importance of race for the study of intergroup relations clearly lies in its social meaning" (1994:23). Marger's is one of the better discussions of the social meanings of race, but I believe his description of the biological confusion about race enhances confusions about the overall meaning of the term.

Schaefer's and Marger's discussions are not adequate correctives to confusions about race: the statement needs to be made that there is only one race, the human race; that there is not and never was a "pure" population, because humans like to travel and breed along the way, and that because there is no such thing as race, it follows that there is no relationship between race and personality.

Schaefer does not mention that the use of the term *race* is confined to biologists discussing genetically isolated animal populations, not humans (and then they prefer *subspecies* over *race* in technical writings, cf. Gould 1977).[2] Nor does Schaefer say that anthropologists have not believed in the idea of pure races for at least a century; further, he seems unaware that in the 1920s the idea of correspondence between physical and cultural traits was rejected. Such discussions as Schaefer's and Marger's, even when motivated by the best possible impulses, are not helpful in eliminating the notion that human races are physical entities or empirical categories. When definitions such as these are given as fact in textbooks, they blur the distinction between popular and scientific definitions and thus indirectly reinforce folk classifications.

Anthropologists, in the meantime, have been investigating the idea of race as a social concept, as a way of categorizing in-groups and out-groups along "color" lines. One of the best illustrations of this point comes from an old episode of "Star Trek." In this story the alien group was one in which all the people were half black and half white. Most were black on the right side, but some were black on the left side. The majority had labeled their mirror images as evil, rebellious, and decidedly inferior. The Enterprise crew encounter these people when they pick up a fugitive and his pursuer; the two have been fighting across the galaxy for centuries and they persist in their fierce battle even after they are returned to their home planet, which has been destroyed by a violent "race" war. Rather than trying to coexist and cooperate as the sole survivors, they continue pursuing one another across the dead planet (Lichter, Lichter, and Rothman 1991:239–240). The message was an encapsulated version of a popular or folk conception of race that is close to the current anthropological view: differences are in the eyes of the beholder, not in the "other" group that in this case was stereotyped as evil, rebellious, and inferior. This is also the liberal version of what television tells us about race relations: "Race shouldn't matter. People are all pretty much alike. They need only emphasize their basic similarities over their superficial differences in order to coexist. . . . No group [is] too different to fit in" (Lichter, Lichter, and Rothman 1991:240). What stands in the way of widespread acceptance of the idea that race doesn't matter? One answer is that social scientists have persisted in assigning some (disputed) reality to definitions of *race*.

Another answer is that differences are construed differently in various societies because the human species is inclined toward classification. Here an analogy with other Western concepts is useful: Mary Douglas (1966) talks about dirt as an idea Westerners impose on external reality in order to make sense of a confusing world. Dirt, she says, is a way of classifying aspects of reality; there is no such thing as "absolute dirt," and the categories of clean and dirty are relative; for example, garden soil is regarded as "clean" until it appears on one's shoes, at which point it is reclassified as "dirt." These reclassifications involve exaggeration of the characteristics of both polar opposites: "It is only by exaggerating the difference between within and without, above and below, male and female, with and against, that a semblance of order is created." (1966:15) "Our classification of what is clean or dirty is a creative attempt to unify experience, a symbolic pattern in which disparate elements are related and disparate experience is given meaning" (Douglas 1966:47).

So, too, with race: our classification of others as members of different races is an attempt to order our social world, to unify our experience into orderly and meaningful sets by classifying people as members of other races, and we simplify the world by subsuming distinctions of class, individual psychology, education, expectations, or income. Such classifications order disparate elements (people) into one or more groups of "others," who are different from "us" by some vague and ill-defined criteria. Schaefer might have done better to say that race is a concept that exists in our minds, not in our bodies.

In the late twentieth-century popular imagination, the idea of distinctive races, with several physical characteristics in common, is giving way to skin color as the criterion. This is partly a result of the failure of attempts such as Jensen's to prove that race and IQ are linked, and partly a result of the elusiveness and difficulty of defining *race* in scholarly, popular, and legal writings. We live in a confusing world: class, ethnicity, and religion give us broad bases for classification, whereas profession, educational background, and political party affiliations are among the narrow bases for classifying others. We have fixed on skin color as one way of sorting out some confusions about who we and they are; this popular "color idiom" is easy, quick, and thoroughly misleading but it follows the principles Douglas suggests: it exaggerates differences and makes the social world more intelligible. Some scholars believe that the American conception of race is a "biracial" one; that is, there are two races, (or skin colors), White and nonwhite (Rodriguez 1989:49). Rodriguez contrasts the American biracial system with the Puerto Rican system of identification, in which both physical and cultural factors were involved:

> Physical and social appearance were the measures used to classify, rather than the biological-descent classification (i.e., "one drop of Negro blood makes you Negro") used in the United States. Thus, in the United States the White-appearing offspring of an interracial couple was classified "Negro." In Puerto Rico, the child would probably have been called White (1989:51–52).

Nor is skin color a negligible criterion.[3] In legal writings, after decades of grappling unsuccessfully with the question of race definitions, the Supreme Court recently treated race and skin color as synonyms:

> An individual juror does not have a right to sit on any particular petit jury, but he or she does possess the right not to be excluded from one on account of race.
> It is suggested that no particular stigma or dishonor results if a prosecutor uses the *raw fact of skin color* to determine the objectivity or qualifications of a juror . . . race cannot be a proxy for determining juror bias or competence (emphasis added, Justice Kennedy in *Powers* v. *Ohio,* 1991:4271).

In the twenty-first century, notions of what constitutes a race will undoubtedly change even more. One recent discovery that may obviate almost all the writings about race that have dominated the last century and a half is the "discovery" of Mitochondrial Eve, a hypothetical woman who lived in Africa somewhere between 90,000 and 180,000 years ago. Biochemists believe that some of "Eve's" descendants eventually left Africa and spread throughout the rest of the world, replacing other populations of humans. They base this idea on studies of mitochondrial DNA, a segment of the DNA molecule inherited only from the mother and altered only by mutations. DNA was taken from human placentas from all parts of the world and used to calculate the number of mutations that had occurred since Eve lived. The most mutations had occurred in the exclusively African sample, suggesting that this was the oldest form of the DNA; the other branches split off later, after the migration out of Africa (Wilson and Cann 1992).

The hypothesis has not gone undisputed (Shreeve 1990; Brown 1990; Thorne and Wolpoff 1992). Scientists question this hypothetical construct for several reasons: first, the theory assumes a steady mutation rate and the accumulation of mutations over generations, an assumption that ignores natural selection's action on mutation; second, the theory ignores the fossil evidence and suggests—by implication—that Eve's descendants, whom Milford Wolpoff calls "killer Africans," may have wiped out all the other hominids in the world. A third reason for doubt is a recent find in China that may point to an East Asian, not African, ancestor (Tianyuan and Etler 1992). Time, and scrupulous scientific investigations, will tell us the truth or falsity of these propositions.

What the Mitochondrial Eve hypothesis means for theories of race is that we are all descended from one (African?) woman, that none of us has pure white ancestry, and that we are more closely related to the rest of the world than "race" theories had suggested previously. The notion of race allowed us to exaggerate the differences between "them" and "us," but the time for such exaggerations is past and we need to reexamine our notions in light of modern understandings of the ideology of racism, to reexamine our beliefs about us/them distinctions in light of mature thinking about differences and similarities, about contradictions and consistencies in our observations.

This book is not an apology for the mistakes of the past, nor is it intended to be a complete account of the history of racist thinking. Instead it is a study in the history of anthropology, one of many social sciences in which individuals have supported their prejudices with "scientific" data and in which concepts are discarded, as race has been in anthropology, when they lose their utility. Stocking, discussing whether the history of anthropological theory is relevant for current theory, notes that "Ultimately, the utility of earlier thinking for present anthropology will have to be judged by the standards of the present. . . . The relevant issue is rather does it help to answer questions which anthropologists are now coping with, or does it help to suggest questions with which they might profitably deal?" (1968:108–109). Both anthropological and popular notions of what constitutes a race have changed dramatically in the last century, but racism has continued to be an important factor in Western societies; I believe this is a question with which anthropologists might—and must—deal. To deal with it, we must go beyond the assertion that there is no such thing as race and talk about what causes us to believe that there is such a thing, about what race as a concept does for "us" as a group, about what racism does to "them" as a group, and what the costs of these beliefs are for the entire society. We also need to think systematically about the most effective means of combating racist ideas, and to train our students to do the same. This cannot be done by simply announcing that anthropologists no longer believe in race.

I have described several instances in which ideas about race changed: ideas about the Irish "race," the invention of slavery for Negroes, Hitler's idea that there was no such thing as race, and the Piltdown example—all illustrate that notions of what constitutes a race and justifications for its use shift according to the economic and political winds. We can now turn to a closer examination of the circumstances in which these notions were first proposed.

DISCUSSION QUESTIONS

1. You are the perpetrator of the Piltdown Hoax. Write a letter to the editor of the leading newspaper in your area, explaining how and why you did it. Note that how it was done is of less interest than why.

2. Lewin mentions two intellectual upheavals in the history of Western philosophy: Copernicus's heliocentric model of the universe and Darwin's model of natural selection. Imagine yourself as a member of the society into which Darwin's theory first came. What kinds of questions might you think it could answer? (Hint: the narrator in John Fowles's novel *The French Lieutenant's Woman* faces these questions.)

3. How many metaphors can you think of that deal with classifying people or things according to their skin color? ("redskins," "white trash," "Black English") How many do you use regularly?

FURTHER READING

The Creation of the Irish "Race"

Two of the best books dealing with English ideas about the Irish "race" are by L. P. Curtis and Richard Ned Lebow; Lebow draws on Curtis's sources, but Curtis's fine style cannot be imitated.

Curtis, L. P., Jr. 1968 *Anglo-Saxons and Celts: A Study of Anti-Irish Prejudice in Victorian England*. Bridgeport, CT: Conference on British Studies at the University of Bridgeport.

Lebow, Richard Ned 1976 *White Britain and Black Ireland: The Influence of Stereotypes on Colonial Policy*. Philadelphia: Institute for the Study of Human Issues.

Two excellent books that deal with American ideas about the Irish (and other immigrant groups) are by Barbara Solomon and Edward Saveth. Saveth's is not as readable as Solomon's. These books are older; newer studies of Irish immigration, such as Diner's, seldom mention the idea of an "Irish" race that was so important in nineteenth-century thought.

Diner, Hasia R. 1983 *Erin's Daughters in America: Irish Immigrant Women in the Nineteenth Century*. Baltimore: The Johns Hopkins University Press.

Saveth, Edward Norman 1948 *American Historians and European Immigrants 1875–1925*. New York: Columbia University Press.

Solomon, Barbara Miller 1956 *Ancestors and Immigrants: A Changing New England Tradition*. Cambridge: Harvard University Press.

Overviews of Race and Slavery

Most of the following are classic studies of American ideas of race and racism from many disciplinary viewpoints. Banton and Harwood's book is one of the last attempts in anthropology to treat the concept of race as a social idea with (possible) biological overtones. Hofstadter considers the whole idea of social Darwinism and its political overtones, and Barzun deals with many historical conceptions of race. Barzun's is the most entertaining of the lot.

My favorite of the current available sociological discussions of race, racism, and institutional racism is Feagin's *Racial and Ethnic Relations*.

Allport, Gordon W. 1958 [1954] *The Nature of Prejudice*. Garden City, NY: Doubleday Anchor and Addison-Wesley.

Banton, Michael and Jonathan Harwood 1975 *The Race Concept*. New York: Praeger.

Barzun, Jacques 1965 *Race: A Study in Superstition*. New York: Harper & Row.

Curtin, Philip D. 1964 *The Image of Africa*. Madison: University of Wisconsin Press.

Feagin, Joe R. 1993 (fourth edition) *Racial and Ethnic Relations*. Englewood Cliffs, NJ: Prentice-Hall.

Gossett, Thomas F. 1963 *Race: The History of an Idea in America*. Dallas: Southern Methodist University Press.

Hofstadter, Richard 1955 [1944] *Social Darwinism in American Thought*. Boston: Beacon Press.

Solomon, Barbara Miller 1956 *Ancestors and Immigrants: A Changing New England Tradition*. Cambridge: Harvard University Press.

Stanton, William 1960 *The Leopard's Spots*. Chicago: University of Chicago Press.

One of the best overviews of the question of slavery is Winthrop D. Jordan's *White Over Black*. Jordan's approach is historical. A recent sociological and comparative view is Orlando Patterson's thoughtful book, *Freedom*, in which he suggests that the emphasis on freedom in Western society was generated by the experience of slavery or serfdom.

Jordan, Winthrop D. 1977 [1968] *White Over Black: American Attitudes Toward the Negro, 1550–1812*.

Patterson, Orlando 1991 *Freedom,* Vol. 1. *Freedom in the Making of Western Culture.* New York: Basic Books.

NOTES

p. 10 1. Herodotus in the fifth century B.C. gave one of the best definitions of this sentiment: "All men, if asked to choose the best way of ordering life, would choose their own." Pierre Van den Berghe (1970:77) credits Ludwig Gumplowicz with coining the term "ethnocentrism" in his 1875 book, *Rasse und Staat.*

p. 16 2. In his textbook, *Sociology,* however, Schaefer does point out that "from a biological perspective, the term *race* would refer to a genetically isolated group with distinctive gene frequencies. It is impossible to scientifically define or identify such a group. Consequently, contrary to popular belief, there are no 'pure races'" (1992:290–291). Further, after noting that some people would like to find biological explanations to understand why some groups dominate others, he says, "Given the absence of pure racial groups, there can be no satisfactory biological answers for such social and political questions." On the same page, he offers a table listing "Racial and Ethnic Groups in the United States, 1990."

p. 18 3. Apparently, skin color is taken very seriously by all Americans. For example, in the entertainment field, a recent op-ed page writer phrased his objections to Sidney Poitier's portrayal of Thurgood Marshall in a TV show in these terms: "The real problem in Mr. Poitier's portrayal is not the difference in the way the two men look. It's the difference in their skin color. Mr. Poitier is very dark and Mr. Marshall very light. . . . The answer for the producers is to cast unknown talented black actors—of which there are many—whose color approximates that of the person portrayed. With black people, skin color counts" (Carter 1991:21).

2

●

The Anthropological Curiosity:
Why Are There Differences?

Progress in the scientific understanding of differences began when the distinction between "how" and "why" questions was clearly drawn and the two kinds of questions and answers were dealt with separately. Several kinds of differences had to be distinguished: those between all living creatures, those between human beings and all other creatures, and those between human beings of different groups. How living creatures are different could be answered with a catalog, listing and describing those differences; why creatures were different was to be answered with the theory of evolution by natural selection. How and why humans differed eventually became the central questions that anthropology sought to answer, both with catalogs and evolutionary theory.

UMBRELLA-FOOTED PEOPLE

Anthropology as a discipline had its formal, scholarly beginnings only a century ago, but its roots lie further back, in the pleasure we all take from tales of how "they" are different from us and in the curiosity that causes us to speculate about the answer to the perennially fascinating question, why are they so different from us? They might be any population, human or animal, but the early travelers told their most entrancing tales about the semihumans they said they encountered. In distant lands, it was reported, people often had two heads or walked on all fours. In the fifth century before Christ, Herodotus (c. 484–425 B.C.) wrote about the "umbrella-footed" people of

Ethiopia, people who could use their (one) foot as a sunshade when the occasion demanded. Herodotus himself had not seen these people but he had been told about them and he noted that these and other strange people, even when they were not so different physically, had very strange habits, such as cannibalism or the worship of "black, mule-nosed gods" (Malefijt 1974:5).

There were physical differences and similarities between creatures, as there were differences and similarities between societies; that much was obvious, but what to make of them, what theory would account for them, was a different matter.

The Greeks were enthusiastic travelers and even more enthusiastic about concocting theories to account for everything they witnessed or were told about. Herodotus believed that the environment was the source of differences, but his contemporary, Empedocles (c. 490–430 B.C.), had a more spectacular theory. Bertrand Russell (1945:54) quotes Empedocles as suggesting that the differences between creatures came after an original scattering of parts: "countless tribes of mortal creatures were scattered abroad endowed with all manner of forms, a wonder to behold."

Russell continued:

There were heads without necks, arms without shoulders, eyes without foreheads, solitary limbs seeking for union. These things joined together as each might chance; there were shambling creatures with countless hands, creatures with faces and breasts looking in different directions, creatures with the bodies of oxen and the faces of men, . . . In the end, only certain forms survived (1945:54).

Both Herodotus and Empedocles explained differences by referring to natural, not supernatural, forces, but each looked at different sorts of phenomena: Herodotus was interested in social differences between human groups, and Empedocles was concerned with physical differences between creatures. In Herodotus's thinking, the environment produced the differences between human societies, whereas in Empedocles's imaginative theory, those physical combinations that were appropriate survived and the inappropriate combinations died out. The random combination of parts explained not only the differences between oxen and humans, but also the existence of the two-headed, four-legged, or umbrella-footed varieties of humankind.

But the theories left many questions unanswered: Herodotus did not tell us exactly how the environment worked to produce differences between societies, nor did Empedocles indicate where the parts came from originally or how, for example, the eye managed to "stray alone" in its search for foreheads. Both thinkers raised as many questions as they answered; but they and others of their time tried to establish what we would now call a scientific explanation of differences, an explanation based on natural—not supernatural—causes. In Greek religion, human societies were the gift of the gods, who transmitted the important inventions to humans, as Prometheus did when he stole fire from Mt. Olympus and shared it with mortals.

Other Greek philosophers agreed with Herodotus that the differences resulted from natural causes, that the environment might have had a large effect on the production of differences. Two sorts of questions can be asked about differences, how and why questions. Herodotus's descriptions of how different "they" were are more flamboyant than his theories about why they were so different, but the Greeks speculated about both kinds of questions. The environment may have produced the differences between the Greeks, the Persians, the Egyptians, and those (sometimes umbrella-footed) Ethiopians who worshipped black, mule-nosed gods (Malefijt 1974:5) or practiced cannibalism, but the specifics of those differences, as well as the ways in which they might have come about, remained unclear.

A century after Empedocles and Herodotus, thinking about the origin and function of differences was stopped cold by Aristotle (384–322 B.C.). Aristotle believed that everything was originally created in the state desired by the Creator and that, although species might deviate from the original design, they did not and could not change their essential form over time. The Christian church adopted Aristotle's position, and in Europe for more than 1,000 years, speculation about evolution was forbidden.

After Aristotle, the search for natural causes of differences was abandoned and "God's will," a supernatural cause, was the answer made to the question, why are there differences? God's will accounted for all, and the spirit of inquiry, though not extinguished, was considerably dampened by those who cried, "Irrelevant" and sometimes "Irreverent" at the inquirers. True believers in God's will might speculate about a "grand design in nature" created by God, but those who looked too closely into that design were suspect for wanting to know exactly how and why the differences had come about, what the mechanisms of differentiation might have been. The story of the Garden of Eden accounted for the physical differences between creatures, which had been created by God, and the Tower of Babel story accounted for the social differences between human groups. Both were the outcome of God's will, and neither was to be questioned.

In the fourteenth and fifteenth centuries, explorations reawakened interest in the question of differences and stimulated a renewed search for natural causes of differentiation, a search for what we would now call scientific answers, signaling that a change in thinking about the world, its many varieties, and its grand design was underway. Differences were again widely reported and speculated on, and even Herodotus's secondhand observations were revived. Sir John Mandeville's work was mostly copied from the writings of the Greek travelers, especially Herodotus, and Mandeville reported, as if he had seen them himself, the existence of a number of strange semi-human creatures, among them, the umbrella-footed people:

> In that country be folk that have but one foot, and they go so blithe that it is marvel, and the foot is so large that it shadoweth all the body against the sun when they will lie and rest them (Mandeville, quoted in Seymour 1968:121–122; first published 1351).

Mandeville piously attributed the differences to God's will, and his fanciful and plagiarized work was more popular in its time than the factual accounts of Marco Polo's trip to China. Marco Polo had seen no strange, semihuman creatures, but the humans he had seen were very different from the Europeans he knew, and he reported the differences as accurately as possible. Mandeville titillated the popular imagination, whereas Marco Polo provided the practical knowledge necessary for further exploration. Under Marco Polo's influence, the first truly scientific coast-charts were drawn up, using collected facts about the known world. Theological and pseudoscientific theories were disregarded and the scientific coast-charts served as guides for later explorers, among them Christopher Columbus (*Encyclopedia Britannica* 1943:174).

Like the ancient Greeks, the European explorers were looking for natural causes of differences. The umbrella-footed people might not be found, but there was considerable variety among those seeming-humans who walked on two legs and had one head: their skin, their hair, and their customs were very different from those Europeans were accustomed to and the differences needed explanation. Mandeville accepted God's will as the complete answer to the questions, whereas Marco Polo reported on how different people were.

Attempts at explanation gave rise to some peculiar theories. One eighteenth-century theorist was Lord Monboddo, whose strange theory suggested that differences between societies could be explained by the "fact" that all humans were born with tails; and different societies developed different ways of concealing tails. Samuel Johnson's comment about Monboddo's theory was that "Other men have strange opinions but manage to conceal them" (quoted in Wolker 1977:252).

Progress in the scientific understanding of differences began in Europe in the seventeenth century, when the founders of modern science began to ask "how" questions: just how different were all living creatures? How could those differences be described? These were not questions that could be answered merely by reference to God's will, nor was it irreverent to speculate about them. The how questions were answered by categorizing and classifying differences between creatures. Linnaeus (1707–1778) provided a preliminary answer by asking the question "How different are all living creatures?" and answering it with a catalog of the differences between them.

Linnaeus's catalog contained many curiosities: in the first edition, he named—but did not further divide—the human species *Homo sapiens* ("wise" or "knowing humans"). In later editions, he divided the human species into four main groups, according to skin color and temperament, and then included some semihumans as near relatives. There were two kinds of semihumans, wild ones and monstrous ones. In the monstrous category were Herodotus's umbrella-footed people because Linnaeus, more than twenty centuries after Herodotus, could not be sure that such people did not exist. Should they exist, should the explorations turn up some umbrella-footed people, there was a category for them in Linnaeus's catalog.

By the nineteenth century, it was fairly clear to scientists that no umbrella-footed people existed. The umbrella-footed people were relegated to fiction and were revived recently for an appearance in one of C. S. Lewis's *Chronicles of Narnia, The Voyage of the Dawn Treader* (1952), where the umbrella-footed people, the Dufflepuds, were described:

> They were certainly very like mushrooms, but far too big—the stalks about three feet high and the umbrellas about the same length from edge to edge. When she looked carefully she noticed too that the stalks joined the umbrellas not in the middle but at one side which gave an unbalanced look to them.
> Each of the 'mushrooms' suddenly turned upside down. The little bundles which had lain at the bottom of the stalks were heads and bodies. The stalks themselves were legs. But not two legs to each body. Each body had a single thick leg right under it (not to one side like the leg of a one-legged man) and at the end of it, a single enormous foot—a broad-toed foot with the toes curling up a little so that it looked rather like a small canoe. . . . They had been lying flat on their backs each with its single leg straight up in the air and its enormous foot spread out above it. . . . the foot kept off both rain and sun . . . (1952:141–142).

The question of the existence of the umbrella-footed people was not resolved until the resurgence of scientific speculation about differences, and anthropology is still heir to both the curiosity and the strange theories that explain differences and similarities; anthropologists still wander in distant lands, seeking answers to questions about differences and similarities among human beings and often broadcasting, rather than concealing, their strange opinions about the causes of those differences.

HOW AND WHY QUESTIONS

Scientific certainty replaced scientific speculation, and answers to the how questions were gathered in all parts of the world. But the scientific certainty was a response to only one sort of question—how different were creatures. The why questions remained a source of speculation. Answers to the how questions could be proved or disproved; answers to the why questions still depend on faith in God's will. The Garden of Eden or the Tower of Babel accounted for the differences between humans, but one could count and describe the differences between other creatures, between dogs and cats or between humans and other primates.

From the how questions came many speculations and many strange theories about the causes, the whys, of differences between species. Even while people were answering the how questions, they were not immune to speculation about why—Linnaeus himself in the first edition of his catalog (1736) included the statement that species could not change, that because they were subject to God's will, they were immutable or unchanging.

After the catalog was published, Linnaeus became famous and people began sending him examples of strange creatures found in different parts of the world. Linnaeus also sent researchers to other parts of the world and as a result of all the new findings, he lost his certainty that species were immutable or unchanging. In the later editions of his catalog (last edition 1758), he removed the assertion that species were unchanging; he did not challenge the Church dogma on this subject, nor did he present any theories to account for the differences, to explain the why of the changes that had occurred in species. He merely removed the statement and left to bolder men the speculation about why changes had occurred.

There were many speculations about the causes of differences between species, many examples of how different creatures had changed. Once the explorers had proved that there were many differences between creatures in different parts of the world, the theory of degeneracy became popular: as creatures had strayed further and further away from the Garden of Eden, their point of origin, they had degenerated by departing from the original type. Comte de Buffon, a proponent of this theory and a Frenchman, assumed that the Garden of Eden must have been very near Paris. Buffon speculated that the farther away from Paris a creature was, the more degenerate it must be, and he described animals in the New World that were puny in size and Indians who were lacking in ardor and unable to impregnate their wives.

In the New World, Thomas Jefferson took issue with Buffon's theory in his *Notes on the State of Virginia* and said that although Buffon believed that American Indians lacked ardor for females, had small organs of generation and little sexual capacity, he (Jefferson) knew that the Indian was "neither more defective in ardor, nor more impotent with his female, than the white reduced to the same diet and exercise" (quoted in Brodie 1974:155). When Jefferson was appointed Ambassador to France, he took along the skins and skeletons of a number of American mammals: deer, elk, and moose, all of them huge. What Buffon said when he was presented with these is not on record, though Jefferson dined with him during the time he was in Paris. Soon there was a theory of "gigantism" that accounted for differences, using much the same logic as the earlier theory of degeneracy, except that the direction of growth was reversed; the farther away from the Garden of Eden, the more gigantic creatures tended to be.

By the end of the eighteenth century, fresh ideas abounded and the search was on for the precise mechanism of change. Scientists were now convinced that species *had* changed—some became extinct, others changed in form— but there was no consensus on why these changes might have taken place. Some thought the Creator had tinkered with his creations or, growing tired of them, had wiped them out and started over again. Others believed the Creator had made species and then left them to fend for themselves, to become degenerate or to flourish.

In contrast, two naturalists, Erasmus Darwin (Charles's grandfather) and Jean Baptiste de Lamarck, suggested that evolution took place when species had to adapt to new environments and that this adaptation took place through the inheritance of favorable characteristics. Further, Erasmus Darwin entertained the outrageous notion that all humans descended from "a common microscopic ancestor."

In the nineteenth century, the most important theory presented to account for differences was the theory of evolution by means of natural selection, a theory proposed by both Charles Darwin and Alfred Russel Wallace almost simultaneously. Evolution, it was suggested, accounted for both the how and the why of species changes, but on different levels.

How did differences between species arise? By means of natural selection or evolutionary differentiation. The theory explained that species had changed according to a very simple mechanism: natural selection, or the forces of the environment, worked on the variability that existed within every species. Darwin and Wallace observed that each species had the ability to reproduce more offspring than were necessary to fill its particular place in the world, and they speculated that the many offspring became fewer, until only those that were well able to survive were left, according to the workings of natural selection. The "fit" survived, and fitness meant that certain individuals were able to produce offspring that would reproduce. Those fit offspring in turn produced others that were fit, and so the process went on. Natural selection, then, was the answer to the question of how differences between species arose, and the emphasis was firmly on the natural, not supernatural, aspects of the process, even though all the mechanics of natural selection were not understood.

Natural selection was a good answer to the how questions; it accounted for the process of differentiation between species. But it was not a good answer to the why questions; natural selection did not explain why particular species arose, nor why some creatures, such as humans, were so very different from others, such as primates. As an answer to the why questions, evolution had certain drawbacks, partly because the theory was not clearly worked out and partly because it allowed no special place for humans. The answers to the how questions could be found by comparing and classifying different species; the answers to the why questions were not so easily found. Why had God or evolution designed or brought into being a world in which there were so many places to be filled and then filled them with the most diverse creatures? Natural selection and environmental forces accounted for that diversity, but not for the special place occupied by humans. Why had God or evolution given dominion over the earth to the human species? As an answer to the how question, evolution involved only natural causes; as an answer to the why question, evolution, like religion before it, sometimes had supernatural overtones.

Darwin and Wallace had both arrived at the answer to the how question of differences between species, but they disagreed on the answer to the why questions. Darwin, who was trained as a theologian but abandoned his faith, disliked speculating about why evolution had occurred and refused to involve himself in discussions of why, of purposes and design in nature. "You are a theologian, I am a naturalist," he once remarked to the vicar of the village in which he lived, "the lines are separate. I endeavour to discover facts without considering what is said in the Book of Genesis. I do not attack Moses, and I think Moses can take care of himself" (Francis Darwin 1898:82–83).

Although Darwin refused to speculate on the "why" of evolution, he took a firm stand on the evolution of the human species by means of natural selection. Humans had evolved just as other animals had; they had not been subject to Divine Intervention or other manifestations of God's will. Wallace, the codiscoverer of natural selection, took the opposite stance and believed that although differentiation among animal species might proceed by natural selection, the evolution of the human species had been guided by supernatural causes, by the Divine Will. To Wallace, human beings were of a different order of creation than the mere beasts, and it followed that humanity had been under the protection of God's will throughout the course of evolution, whereas those animals that lacked souls had been subject to natural selection. The Creator must have overseen the evolution of humanity and left the other animals to sort things out for themselves according to the principles of natural selection. Darwin maintained his beliefs in natural causes to the end of his life; he believed in scientific questions and answers and he did much to establish the how questions as the principle endeavors of those who studied any aspect of nature. Wallace, on the other hand, became so involved in speculations about spiritual matters that he forsook the how questions and the scientific quest in order to learn more about the "why" of human existence. While Darwin gathered to himself a group of scientists who continued to investigate evolutionary processes, Wallace attended seances and dabbled in the occult. Darwin's concerns and convictions carried the day, and it is Darwin who is remembered for the "discovery" of the principles of natural selection.

The disagreement between Darwin and Wallace about the merit of asking how and why questions exemplifies their century; Wallace sought to reconcile his version of evolution by natural causes with God's will as the ultimate explanation. Darwin sought to establish the how questions as questions worth asking, and to leave alone the why questions that could not be answered, except by speculation. Wallace's thinking was in many ways the final attempt in the nineteenth century to reconcile supernatural and natural causes; Darwin's thinking initiated the twentieth century's emphasis on natural causes.

Many who came after Darwin were, like Darwin himself, "converted" from a supernatural explanation to a natural explanation of the variety around them. It is not surprising, then, that those who sought natural explanations for differences used evolution or natural selection in much the same manner as the theologians had used the phrase *God's will* before them. Evolution could be made to account for everything: like God's will before it, evolution accounted for the birds and the bees and the beasts of the field. The "grand design in nature" that could be perceived even by a casual observer could be a product only of evolution or of a Divine Creator.

The evolutionists were as rabid in their application of evolutionary theory as those who believed in God's will had been before them. With a nearly Inquisitorial fervor, the converts to evolutionary theory applied their ideas. Their zeal illustrates what Kaplan calls the Law of the Instrument: if you give a small boy a hammer, he will soon discover that everything in sight needs pounding (Kaplan 1964:28). Every explanation in sight, every question that could be asked, was soon pounded with the evolutionary hammer.

EVOLUTION

Explanations that had previously depended on God's will were redrafted in evolutionary terms. During the latter half of the nineteenth century, evolution was the answer to both how and why questions, and evolution, not God, had made things as they were. Evolution accounted for the differences between oxen and humans, as well as for the differences between human groups. Applying evolution to social phenomena also gave Westerners a clear explanation of their own superiority over the rest of the world: Europeans, in Linnaeus's terms had been "light, lively and inventive"; other groups were phlegmatic or dull or lacking in ardor. The explanation for the superiority of Europeans over the other races lay in their being more highly evolved than the others. Whites were the most highly evolved race and their evolutionary blessings allowed them to assume their "natural" place as world leaders and conquerors.

In the early days of applying evolutionary theory to everything, the mechanics of the evolutionary process were not well understood. If anything, this made it easier to apply the theory to everything, and Darwin's own confusion about some aspects of the process probably contributed to the misunderstandings and misinterpretations. Darwin and his contemporaries were uncertain about the mechanics of inheritance; what they were certain of was that adaptation was the end product of evolution, that successful species were adapted to a particular environment.

Earlier observers had believed that adaptations were a product of the grand design in nature, but Darwin's contribution to science was to suggest a model by which the adaptations must have come into being. The model involved two forces: one for stability and one for variation (Alland 1967:119).

Over time, the two forces in combination caused the seemingly miraculous "fit" between an organism and its environment. Those animals that were not well suited to an environment left few offspring, while those that were well suited left many offspring. If the environment changed, then the chances of a group's survival might be increased or decreased. By a balance between the forces working toward stability or variation, a population could adapt to changing circumstances, could maintain its adaptation in stable circumstances or, if the population could not adapt, it would go to extinction.

Darwin's followers, who were no more able than he to find a satisfactory solution to the question of inherited variations, emphasized or overemphasized the idea of stability, and it was an idea well suited to political aims. Those who applied Darwin's theory to everything preferred to concentrate their energies in working out the dynamics of the stabilizing forces, the conservative forces in nature. The conservative forces appealed to those who wished their own superiority underlined by scientific, natural principles. As the end product of evolutionary forces that molded species and chose the "best," the upper classes were naturally superior to the lower classes, just as military victors were naturally superior to those they vanquished. Evolution, not God, had designed it that way. Because the laws of inheritance were not understood nor, accordingly, the origins of diversity within a species, the force for stability in Darwin's theory was elaborated as an explanation for the why questions about differences. Those who asked how questions were often convinced, too, that Evolution was the complete explanation for the why questions, even though the how questions were not fully answered. Faith in Evolution meant that the questions would in time be answered.

Anthropology had its formal beginnings as a discipline during this period (1860–1900), and the evolutionary hammer was applied to concepts that had previously been used to describe differences among human populations. Two classificatory devices were used, concepts that could be used in tandem to describe all the differences that existed within the human species. These concepts were race and culture. Race was a well-developed concept in natural history before it was taken over by anthropology and wherever it was used, it had strong ethnocentric overtones; that is, those who used it always classified their own group as the superior one, all others as inferior. Linnaeus had classified the varieties of human beings according to a fourfold classification that included temperamental differences such as "light and lively" as part of the inherent nature of each racial group. Other groups were "choleric" or "lazy" or some such derogatory term. Aristotle, a member of what he called the Hellenic race, did the same:

> Those who live in a cold climate, such as Europe, are full of spirit but wanting in intelligence and skill. Those who live in Asia are intelligent and inventive but are wanting in spirit. The Hellenic race, however, situated between the two, is likewise intermediate in character, being high-spirited and also intelligent (paraphrased from Aristotle).

Another kind of social theory flourished at the end of the nineteenth century, when anthropology had its disciplinary beginnings: it was called *social Darwinism*, but it was the invention of Herbert Spencer, the "father of sociology" and an admirer of Darwin. Spencer believed that Darwinian principles of natural selection could be seen to be operating in human society; he coined the phrase "survival of the fittest" (which was used by Darwin subsequently) and he meant by it that in every society, those who are at the top (socially, economically, or politically) are fittest or best, and those who are indigent or otherwise underprivileged are the least fit or worst. Considering English society against others, this meant that the "fittest" nation had triumphed over other, less-fit nations; considering English social classes, it meant that the aristocracy and the middle class were better or more fit than those who had no access to privilege and power. The implicit ethnocentrism of this theory must have been highly satisfactory to those who propounded it, for it explained why they were the victors in some long past social struggle and lent "scientific credence" to their belief in their own superiority.

Culture was not so well developed a concept as race, but both concepts brought along legacies from past thinkers. With race, the legacy was a propensity for categorizing and classifying in a hierarchical way, that is, A is better than B and B is better than C, and so on. With culture, the legacy was a propensity for romanticizing the lifeways of other groups, for looking at "primitive" peoples and seeing in them the childhood of European civilizations or the ideal, unspoiled character of the "noble savage." Anthropology took the whole of humanity as its special sphere of interest; human beings in all times and places could be accounted for by evolution—in the vaguest and most theological sense of that term—and race and culture were the two concepts to be used in exploring the question of how human beings came to be different or, how "they" came to be different from us.

Race and culture were the dual cornerstones on which the discipline was founded. Human beings were either innately, physically different (race) or they were different because they had learned different habits (culture). These two concepts became the basis of further studies: they were analytic concepts, or informing, working concepts that allow further investigation. Class is such a concept in sociology, as is mind in psychology. As analytic concepts intended to shed light on the nature of differences, on the how questions about human differences, race and culture covered all the possibilities. Race and culture were not carefully separated early on; separating them was to be the work of future generations of anthropologists.

The ultimate explanation for human differences was evolution and the emphasis on evolution's conservative force made the study of differences simpler than it might otherwise have been. All characteristics could be ranked according to the resemblance they bore to European characteristics. If "we" were civilized, "they" were savages—or perhaps barbarians, if we were kindly disposed toward them. If we practiced monogamy, they must be promiscuous or given to marrying many wives. Intellectually and emotionally, these theories must have been as satisfying to their adherents as God's will had been to the faithful in earlier centuries. But those who used evolution as the answer to the why questions and adopted race and culture as answers to the how questions ignored, at their peril, the other evolutionary force Darwin posited, the force for variation, and variation is the subject of the next chapter. It was not that Darwin himself was uninterested in variation; he was, on the contrary, "obsessed" with it, in Gould's phrase. Darwin's followers, especially those social Darwinists who wanted to find biological reasons for all social phenomena, concentrated on stability.

It was in this spirit that anthropology, as a scholarly discipline, had its beginnings. The differences between creatures could be studied scientifically; that is, differences could be accounted for by natural causes. The Garden of Eden and the Tower of Babel were banished as explanations and differences were to be studied according to the new scientific procedures, the search for causes of differences in which evolution was the answer to both how and why questions. Gould (1979:26) says that evolutionary biology is the science of why questions; anthropology, by and large, has continued as one of the social sciences that addresses itself to how questions, to exploring and describing human differences both within the species and between the human species and others.

EVOLUTION ANSWERS HOW AND
WHY QUESTIONS ABOUT DIFFERENCES

Descartes observed about knowledge that if the first button be wrongly done up, then so will all the others. The first button we must be concerned with is the concept of evolution, and this must be clearly and rightly done up before going on. That is, to understand the uses and misuses of Darwinian theory in explaining human differences, we must look at evolution as it is currently understood both by scientists and in the popular imagination. In its broadest sense, evolution refers to the proposition that all organisms are related and that change has occurred by means of natural forces that have operated in the process of differentiation (Eldredge and Tattersall 1982:2). Or, as Stephen Jay Gould puts it, "Evolution, to professionals, is adaptation to changing environments, not progress" (Gould 1989:32).

This is the professional, not the popular, concept of evolution: many people understand evolution to mean progressive improvement, often through the inheritance of acquired (useful) characteristics. This is the way in which Lamarck thought evolution operated. Opposite the entrance to the college in which I teach is a church with a signboard outside, and each week they post different sayings on the signboard. One of their favorites is "If Evolution works, why don't mothers have three hands?" This idea about how evolution "works" (or doesn't) is a Lamarckian idea with some social Darwinist frills, and it reflects a common misunderstanding of the process of evolutionary differentiation. Some of Lamarck's ideas are often mistaken for Darwinian evolutionary principles, and Darwin himself occasionally made use of Lamarckian principles. Among these are several erroneous notions: the belief that only the fittest survive; the notion that evolution selects progressively better organisms in a striving for perfection; and the idea that "we" are the end product of a long evolutionary process that causes us and others like us to be the beneficiaries of all the best traits available to a species (Degler 1991:24; cf. Bleibtreu and Meaney 1973).

These ideas may be part of the current, popular conception of evolution, but they do not describe the process of evolutionary change or differentiation between species as scientists now understand it, nor indeed as scientists have understood it for almost a century. The current debate among scientists has to do with the timing of the forces that bring about differentiation: some believe that those forces operate rapidly (punctuated equilibrium), others that the forces operate slowly and uniformly (Darwinians). No scientist now believes that the forces have operated deliberately (Lamarckians) to "perfect" a species.

To describe the various theories of differentiation, we can use the example of giraffes, the example that is most often used in discussion of Lamarck's ideas. As it happens, Lamarck himself never discussed giraffes, but they are useful for illustrating various current ideas about evolution. We will talk about three main ways of dealing with questions about variation and stability:

> *Popular, sometimes called Lamarckian*: strivings produced a gradual change toward the better, thus the "better" animals survived.

> *Darwinian*: stability and variation produced slow, gradual changes; environment selected the fittest organisms.

> *Punctuated equilibrium or "new biology"*: variation and stability allow adaptation to occur; rapid change due to environmental shifts.

First, we must define our terms and set the scene. We are looking at the evidence for changes in species over time and we want to know how those changes have occurred, specifically how one ancestral species might lead to two new species. *Speciation* is the technical name given to the process by which new species arise, the process in which two species are formed from one ancestral species. A *species* is an interbreeding group or a population, any of whose members can, theoretically, breed with any other member and produce viable offspring, that is, offspring that can reproduce themselves. A *subspecies* is a part of that overall population whose members can interbreed but seldom do, usually for reasons of geography, sometimes behavior. Horses and donkeys are separate species, though they must have been subspecies at some time past. They can interbreed but they do not produce viable offspring. Instead, they produce mules, a sterile group. So horses and donkeys are different species, two separate groups that cannot interbreed and produce viable offspring.

One of the best examples of speciation is the process by which giraffes and okapis were differentiated from their common ancestor, which we will call a "pregiraffe."

A "pregiraffe" is called by scientists a "primitive giraffe," *Paleotraginae*, (Grzimek 1972:246). The scientific discussion of differences and similarities between fossil and living giraffes and okapis is summarized in C. S. Churcher (1978:509–535), and also reviewed in Singer and Bone (1960:375–603) and Geraads (1986:465–477). The okapi (*Okapia johnstoni*) was first described scientifically in 1901 by E. Ray Lankester (1901:279–314). Henry Morton

Stanley, in his explorations of the Congo, recorded talk of a "donkey," later called a "forest horse," and his description of the animal drew the attention of Sir Harry Johnston, then governor of Uganda. Johnston searched unsuccessfully for the animal but managed to buy some skins from the Mbuti Pygmies of the area, and he sent the skins to London, where they were first thought to belong to a new species of horse. When two skulls arrived a year later, the animal was identified as a relative of an extinct, short-necked giraffe and given its name, okapi, from an Mbuti word.

Our pregiraffe, which lived in the Miocene, about twenty-five million years ago, looked more like the present-day okapis than giraffes do (see Figure 1). Okapis are small creatures, standing about five feet at the shoulder. Their necks are not overly elongated but are "in proportion" to the rest of their bodies, in much the same way that an antelope's neck is to its body. Both okapis and giraffes are browsing animals by preference, that is, they eat leaves, but the okapi is better equipped for eating low and medium bushes or trees than the giraffe.

Our next step, then, in studying speciation is to imagine that we can go back in time, find the ancestral population of pregiraffes, follow the herd around for many millions of years, and see exactly how speciation occurred, how the pregiraffes got differentiated into two populations, one of okapis and one of giraffes. When we arrive to begin studying our herd of pregiraffes, we notice that there are differences between them. Some have short necks, some have medium necks, and some have long necks; some have short tails, medium tails, and long tails; others have short eyelashes, medium eyelashes, and long eyelashes. What are we to make of those differences? We will consider them in three different ways: the popular or Lamarckian way, the Darwinian way, and the punctuated equilibrium way.

In the popular/Lamarckian version, the herd of pregiraffes would contain some individuals that stretched their necks to reach the highest treetops, to browse from food that was out of the reach of other members of the herd. These pregiraffes had discovered that the best food was in the taller trees and they kept on trying to reach the higher branches. This neck-stretching characteristic was passed on to the offspring and after centuries of trying, the pregiraffes evolved into giraffes, the "best" of their species. The Lamarckian idea is the inheritance of acquired characteristics; in the popular version, which draws on social Darwinist ideas, value judgments are added. So there are giraffes in the world today because the "best" pregiraffes were selected out of all possible pregiraffes, on the basis of only one characteristic, neck length, and the continued attempt to stretch their necks, which was passed on to the offspring (see Figure 2).

In the popular or Lamarckian theory, then, the explanation of the *differences* that *exist* is that they are there *to help create better species*. There are two problems, however: first, there are okapis in the world, and according to the theory, there should not be, because okapis are the descendants of the "inferior" animals, the ones that did not try harder, and the ones that did try are the giraffes, the "better" species.

The second problem is that the evidence indicates that higher animals do not inherit acquired characteristics, that is, characteristics that the parents acquire during their lifetime, from their parents.

This popular version of evolution has the character of a Kipling "Just So" story; in the same way that the Elephant Child got his long nose (trunk) from his struggle to pull his initially short nose out of the jaws of the Crocodile, the pregiraffes got their long necks from their struggles to stretch upward toward the more delicious leaves. Although both the popular version and Kipling's may be charming, neither is correct, and in the case of the giraffes, the facts are far more interesting than the fiction.

Now let's go on to the Darwinian version of how the change took place. It is much the same scenario but there are some changes. We are still looking at the same herd of pregiraffes during the same several million years. There are still differences within the herd, some with short necks, others with long necks (and tails and eyelashes), but all are members of the same breeding population, the population of pregiraffes.

Darwin saw that within any given species, more offspring were produced than would survive to reproductive age, and from this, he assumed that the environment was gradually selecting out the most "fit" of the animals to survive. All of the pregiraffes would do a lot of browsing, feeding on low, medium, and tall bushes or trees. Now let us suppose that during the period in which we were following our pregiraffes, we saw a gradual change in the environment, a change that took place very slowly, one that caused all the medium bushes to disappear. The animals that survived this change would gradually be separated into two groups: short-necked pregiraffes that fed on low bushes and long-necked pregiraffes that fed on high trees (see Figure 3). The transitional forms might be intermediate between okapis and giraffes, but if they had medium-sized necks and the food for medium-necked pregiraffes disappeared, this group would be at a disadvantage. In the Darwinian version, the environment weeds out the least fit of the group and leaves the others, so the medium-necked (transitional) forms would disappear. The gradual changes in the environment would cause the animals to split into two populations, and those two populations, due to environmental change or to geographical separation, would eventually become okapis and giraffes.

In this explanation, *differences exist* in order *to better adapt the animals to their (slowly changing) environment,* and the slow, cumulative changes may one day produce a new creature. But there are still problems with the explanation. What Darwin could not understand or explain was why, once the separation had occurred, there were still variations within successful (fit) members of the population. Why did the variations persist after the two species were clearly established? Why would medium-necked animals continue to be born? Darwin considered that perhaps in rare circumstances, a really extraordinary creature must

FIGURE 1 *A giraffe and an okapi.*

have been produced, what is called a *mutation*, and that this "hopeful monster," as one theorist termed the mutations, might succeed in producing offspring.

To answer the objections raised to the Darwinian theory, let's go on to the third version, the punctuated equilibrium version: suppose that while we were following the pregiraffes around, we saw a "sudden" change in the environment, a change that took place over a period of several thousand years and again caused all the medium bushes to disappear, but quickly, not slowly as in the Darwinian case. Soon after, we might notice that there were differences between the pregiraffes, differences that caused them to favor slightly different environments (see Figure 4). The differences, however, would not prevent them from interbreeding: these would be "racial" or "subspecific" differences, and in and of themselves, relatively meaningless. If the environment were to favor the growth of medium bushes once again, the differences would probably disappear. If, however, the environment continued to "favor" those with long necks for browsing in high trees and those that browsed on low bushes, then the two "racial" groups would eventually seek different areas and there gradually adapt more completely to their respective environments, until the differences between the two populations became so great over time as to prevent them from interbreeding.

For the two populations to become separated, several factors might intervene: the medium bushes might disappear completely, causing the short-necked pregiraffes to go off in one direction in search of more low bushes,

FIGURE 2 *The Lamarckian theory of evolution.*

and the long-necked to go in a different direction in search of tall trees. Or a small group of the pregiraffes could become separated from the main group and have to adapt to the new environment, drawing on the genetic variation that was available within its segment of the population. In the new biology version, *differences exist to allow the species to survive in the face of unpredictable, often rapid, changes in environment.*

Now if we go through this scenario once more, this time adding a committee of medium-necked, medium-tailed, and medium-eyelashed social Darwinist pregiraffes, it is easy to see how some of these versions of evolutionary change lent themselves to racist, discriminatory thinking. To a social Darwinist pregiraffe, the differences among pregiraffes might reflect the inner strivings of the population that were there to help create a better species. Because the "best" pregiraffes were those that were medium in all respects, those that had long or short characteristics would be considered imperfect members of the species. Social Darwinists pushed Darwinian theory a step beyond its original claims by insisting that physical characteristics were indicators of the "progress" a species had made, so our social Darwinist pregiraffes might decide to eliminate (prevent from breeding) those animals that had "inferior" neck, tail, or eyelash lengths, that is, those that differed from their own ideas about what was perfect. Remember that Hitler said he wanted to create the "perfect race," to establish racial purity and rid the country/world of those impure members of the human species (even though, as we have

FIGURE 3 *The Darwinian theory of evolution by differential reproduction.*

seen, his real interest was in finding a basis for uniting the German people, not in racial purity). But this kind of theory was regularly applied to human races in the nineteenth century and is still applied to them on occasion; Europeans were the race that tried hardest, and the others were merely losers, inferior specimens, in some grand cosmic game.

In the Darwinian version, diversity exists so that creatures can adapt to their slowly changing environment. To justify human racial discrimination is more subtle in these terms, but with an emphasis on the forces for stability, not variation, at work in the evolutionary process, differences—in whatever selected characteristic—can be seen as indicative of inferior status. Then the argument runs like this: those members of the species who have this characteristic are "inferior" and, if the normal forces of selection were working properly, they could not survive to adulthood. Normal selection forces are interfered with by charity, or by remedial programs aimed at giving the "inferior" members equal opportunity. This rationale was and is used by social Darwinists as a justification for sterilizing members of the (human) population considered unfit, that is, the feebleminded, the blacks who overproduced themselves, and so on.

The punctuated equilibrium version is the only one that makes allowance for giraffes and okapis by assuming that the diversity that exists within populations will permit the population to survive in different conditions, especially to survive extreme changes in conditions. Things may stay more or less the same over millions of years and then change abruptly. So this third ver-

FIGURE 4 *The theory of punctuated equilibrium.*

sion, the new biology version, would account for speciation of the pregiraffes as a process that happened rapidly, due to extreme climatic changes, and two populations, giraffes and okapis, survived.

Evolution, or natural selection, then, does not lead to progressive betterment of species. It leads to the multiplication of species, some of which will become extinct and others of which will survive. This is not the same thing as "survival of the fittest," or progressive betterment of the species, because it is the variability within a species—the differences between the parents and the offspring in the case of the pregiraffes—that enables a species or more than one species to survive and to adapt. The "fittest" pregiraffes, before the environmental shift, would have been those with medium-length necks for browsing on low, medium, and tall bushes. The forces for stability worked for the medium-necked pregiraffe so long as the environment was constant. In a changing environment, the forces for variation enabled the population—but not the medium-necked pregiraffes—to adapt to the changes.

I have said that not all aspects of this process were clear to Darwin. He understood that there were forces for stability and for variation in every population, and that the interaction of the two forces produced the seemingly miraculous fit between an organism and its environment. He did not understand how the forces for variation and for stability (the mechanisms of inheritance) were retained in a population, but it was clear that Darwin's version of how evolution worked was able to answer more questions about species differentiation than the Lamarckian version that preceded it.

Evolution selects those individuals that are suited for a particular environment. This is not a moral or a philosophic judgment about which individuals are best. It is a temporary state of affairs, based on both stability and variation. Indeed, a "pure" population, one that contained only those characteristics best suited to the current environment, might not be able to survive a change in that environment. Like the pregiraffes, the population that could survive would be the one that had mixed characteristics, including some characteristics that were helpful in a new environment.

If the environment is unchanging, then the selection process will operate in favor of those individuals that are well adapted within that environment, but the variation available to the population will not be entirely lost. However, if the circumstances should change drastically, the population may not have a sufficient amount of variability within it to meet that change; should the tall trees disappear from the open plains and the giraffes be forced to return to grazing, they might not be able to survive that shift. But if they did survive it, they would not return to being okapis. The new species would be short-necked giraffes.

These are the explanations for how evolution or natural selection operates. It does not select only the "fittest," for fitness is always a relative term, relative to the environment at the moment. Nor does selection work with some grand design or purpose, against which inferior or different individuals are always being tested. Which individuals survive depends on the conditions of this moment and the next, not on some preordained plan.

Because environments are always changing, survival of the fittest is not a helpful concept, for it works only in a specific environment for a short period of time. Evolution does not select progressively better organisms in a striving for perfection; the selecting forces are quite random, depending on the environment at the moment and on the organism's ability to generate diversity in offspring. Human beings, like giraffes, are not the end products of a long evolutionary process that causes them to be the beneficiaries of all the best traits available to a species; they are the products of evolution, of evolutionary variation and responses to particular environments, of which differences are one sort of response a species can make to varying environments. These differences are minor episodes in the adaptive process.

With that first button, the concept of evolution, done up properly, now we can go back to the question of Evolution in its quasi-theological sense, as the answer to the why questions. Why were human beings so different from the rest of the animal kingdom? In the Lamarckian version, humans were different because Evolution had selected progressively better organisms in a striving for perfection. Darwin comes close, in *The Descent of Man*, to saying just this when he is discussing the evolution of the moral faculties. But in the Darwinian version, evolution had molded the mainly physical characteristics of one group of primates in such a way that those primates became protohumans. This was not a foreordained plan, nor an instance of predestination because of inner strivings; it was an accident of adaptation, the culmination of a series of minute adaptive steps that were responses to specific environmental conditions. Humans were slightly different from other creatures because of their unique evolutionary history, but the differences, Darwin argued, between humans and other primates were minor and sometimes minute. Subsequent research has proved him right.

Humans then were different because they, like other creatures, had responded to their environment, but they had adapted to slightly different material forces than other species and they had evolved, somewhere along the line, what we now call *culture*, a different set of abilities, learned abilities, that allowed them to bypass many of the problems that other animals might face. Polar bears, facing increasingly cold environments, evolved or developed long fur; humans invented clothes. In the next chapter, we will see how Charles Darwin and Alfred Russel Wallace viewed the different lifeways of the groups they saw on their travels and how they analyzed those differences, mostly without the emphasis on learning that we now associate with culture.

DISCUSSION QUESTIONS

1. Glyn Isaac stated that "Regardless of how scientists present them, accounts of human origins are read as replacement materials for Genesis. They . . . do more than cope with curiosity, they have allegorical content, and they convey values, ethics, and attitudes" (quoted in Lewin 1989:1). What are some of these allegorical contents, and what values, ethics, and attitudes are being conveyed?

2. In your view, is "man's place in nature" rightly regarded as being somehow special? Do Herodotus's and Empedocles's ideas agree with this? Imagine yourself debating this notion with an environmentalist who is concerned about saving the spotted owl or some other endangered species.

3. Imagine you are a judge in the "Most Beautiful Okapi" contest and must select among a wide variety of contestants. Explain how you would make this choice if you were (1) a social Darwinist; (2) a punctuated equilibriumist.

FURTHER READING

The best discussion of notions of savages is Margaret T. Hodgen's.

Hodgen, Margaret T. 1964 *Early Anthropology in the Sixteenth and Seventeenth Centuries*. Philadelphia: University of Pennsylvania Press.

For a review of the development of evolutionary theory, Loren Eiseley's *Darwin's Century* and Jacques Barzun's *Darwin, Marx, Wagner* are classics and well worth reading, as are Stephen Jay Gould's recent articles on aspects of Darwinian theory, especially *Ever Since Darwin* and *Wonderful Life*.

Barzun, Jacques 1958 *Darwin, Marx, Wagner*. Garden City, NY: Anchor Books.

Eiseley, Loren 1961 *Darwin's Century: Evolution and the Men Who Discovered It.* Garden City, NY: Anchor Books.

Gould, Stephen Jay 1977 *Ever Since Darwin.* New York: W. W. Norton.

———— 1989 *Wonderful Life: The Burgess Shale and the Nature of History.* New York: W. W. Norton.

3

●

Ignoble Savages or Just Others?
Charles Darwin and
Alfred Russel Wallace

This chapter contrasts the attitudes of Charles Darwin and Alfred Russel Wallace, codiscoverers of the principle of natural selection, toward the differences between themselves and the indigenous peoples they came into contact with during their travels. Darwin and Wallace held disparate views about the differences between themselves and others—Wallace believing that the mental differences were minor, Darwin that differences were major, and that if those major differences were not fixed or permanent, then they were a product of the gradual evolution of the brain. Darwin's ideas about human differences, based in part on the social Darwinist ideas of Herbert Spencer, triumphed, at least until the mid-twentieth century.

Charles Darwin's vision of the workings of natural selection had great impact on twentieth-century thought, and his views on evolution have led to many reconsiderations of the place of humans in nature. As one of the nineteenth century's three most influential thinkers (the other two are Marx and Freud), and author of the twentieth century's scientific paradigm, it is not surprising that nearly every aspect of Darwin's life—his personality, his early childhood, his illnesses—has been examined and reexamined at enormous length (see Further Reading). Darwin's views on all subjects were taken seriously, but, paradoxically, his view of human beings and his ethnocentric ideas about other cultures have seldom been considered systematically or critically by historians of science. These ideas are most easily examined by contrasting Darwin's views with those of Alfred Russel Wallace, one of the few contemporaries who dared to disagree with Darwin about the nature of other human groups and the meaning of differences. Both men wrote journals of their travels and those journals reveal many differences in their approaches, differences that continued to influence the popular images of other peoples, other cultures, throughout their lifetimes and well into our own century. Darwin authored the scientific paradigm of the twentieth century and influenced the development of social Darwinism, together with its racist policies, whereas Wallace anticipated the nonracist view of other cultures that anthropologists now accept.

For this alone, it would be worthwhile to reexamine Darwin's and Wallace's views, but there is another, equally compelling reason: as we seek to know more about our great scientists, we may find mistaken confirmation of our own opinions in theirs. Thus, Darwin's abhorrence of slavery, especially for Negroes, is often mentioned, but his mild disapproval of genocidal wars against Native Americans and his suggestion that slavery might not be too hard on Native Americans are bypassed. Wallace spent years living with the native peoples of South America and the Pacific, in much the same fashion that later ethnographers would aspire to, and he wrote liberally about the many things he had learned from looking at the natives' point of view; yet he also wrote in the most damning terms of the savagery and brutality of these people. The views expressed in both men's journals were predicated on their prior convictions, that is, they saw what they expected to see. Darwin held to a highly Eurocentric view, judging other cultures according to their similarity or difference with his beloved England; Wallace adhered to a highly relativistic view, in which he forbore making judgments about the indigenous cultures he saw, though he never hesitated to state his disapproval of the European settlers he came into contact with.

DARWIN AND THE IGNOBLE SAVAGES

Darwin spent nearly five years at sea on the voyage of *HMS Beagle* and came into close contact with many inhabitants of South America, Tahiti, Australia, and New Zealand. His journal of the voyage of the *Beagle* was a popular success when it was first published in 1839; in it, he recorded his observations on all manner of natural phenomena and speculated about whether the progenitors of civilized human beings could have been like those savage creatures he had seen with his own eyes. In 1871, when he published *The Descent of Man*, it was clear that the intervening thirty-two years had not improved Darwin's image of "the savage." Once again he speculated about our barbarian progenitors and this time expressed his own preference for being descended from a baboon.

Several things are noticeable in Darwin's writings about other cultures. First, he was quite ethnocentric and believed firmly that the English way of life was the very best way of life ever devised by human beings. Second, he was a believer in facial expressions as indicators of character, a common belief in the nineteenth century but one not popular today. Third, Darwin was inclined to hero-worship, especially of those in authority, and this inclination often led him astray in his estimation of the character of others. Fourth, in much the same way that Irene Adler was *The* Woman for Sherlock Holmes, for Darwin, *The* Savage was the Tierra del Fuegian. Fifth, in both *The Voyage of the Beagle* (hereafter *Voyage*) and *The Descent of Man* (hereafter *Descent*), Darwin's references to savages are almost invariably followed by references to lower animals: he equates the language of savages with the noise made when calling chickens, and suggests that there is as much difference between civilized and primitive humans as between domesticated and wild animals. Finally, Darwin seems never to have grappled with culture shock, the syndrome that afflicts travelers who encounter strange customs (Oberg 1954). Most people, especially when they stay for a long time in a foreign place, come to terms with foreign customs and with other people's ideas and lifeways. In Darwin's time, few travelers stayed long enough in places inhabited by "savage" peoples to go all the way through the phases of culture shock. Some individuals, however, particularly those insulated from daily life as others live or see it, never do come to terms with strange customs and practices. Darwin, by reason of his upper middle-class upbringing and his position as gentleman-naturalist on the *Beagle*, was one of those who never came to terms, never grappled with the strangeness of other lifeways; Wallace, a poorer man who earned a living by selling specimens to wealthy European collectors, was forced to live with the "natives" and was interested in learning their languages, in hearing their ideas about the strange specimens he had been sent to capture. Wallace, unlike Darwin, did pass through all the stages of culture shock, arriving at the final stage of cultural relativism fairly early in his life.

The stages of culture shock are, first, the "rose-colored glasses" stage in which other customs are seen as delightful, much more free or appealing than the ones the individual is familiar with. In the second stage, the individual is angry and disoriented; strange customs seem inexplicable or whimsical or foolish. The third stage brings a kind of bitter humor or sarcasm, in which the individual pokes fun at the customs of the host group.

The final stage brings the realization that the host group's lifeways are different—not better, not worse—just different. (Many of my students report a mild form of culture shock on leaving high school and entering college, where the norms and expectations are often quite different.) This mature, nonjudgmental stage, known as cultural relativism, allows people to adapt to a different culture and to learn about that culture without forcing its members or customs into stereotypical molds. What is often not said in discussions of cultural relativism is that one may never come to like a particular group or to appreciate all its customs. It is necessary to suspend judgments, not preferences or deeply felt moral convictions. Cultural relativists may make informed decisions, in which they look at the good and the bad with a "measured eye," not decisions based on ignorance, stereotyping, or the repetition of xenophobic or ethnocentric notions. This fourth stage of tolerance and understanding is the stage Darwin seems never to have reached in his travels; throughout his writings, his views of other human groups are informed by stereotypes, big-otry, and failures of understanding. With the Gauchos—the only group in whose company he spent any appreciable time—he came closest, and offered the opinion that they were gentlemen, although cutthroats.

In Darwin's defense, it must be said that there was no such thing as ethnography, the systematic description of other lifeways, in his time. Whether Darwin's descriptions inhibited the development of ethnography is unknowable, but few readers would have come away from his work fired with curiosity about other lifeways and other human groups. Although there were not many systematic descriptions of other human groups in the 1830s, there were a great many unsystematic accounts; these often blended fact and fiction according to the author's whim, but Darwin avoided repeating many of the fictions he must have heard. Darwin was a good observer and, had it not been for his ethnocentrism, he might have provided a more sympathetic account of the natives he saw; as it was, he sought to describe what he saw scientifically and in the terms of natural history, as when he describes a young man as a "good specimen of a wild Brazilian youth" (*Voyage*:27).

THE VOYAGE OF THE *BEAGLE*

In December 1831, when Darwin embarked on *HMS Beagle*, he was only a few weeks away from his twenty-second birthday. He was the "gentleman naturalist" (the ship's surgeon, Robert McKormick, was also a naturalist) on the *Beagle*'s scientific expedition to little-known parts of the world, and Darwin had two tasks: first, to serve as dinner companion to the captain, who could not mix with the crew; and second, as geologist-naturalist, to catalog, classify, and describe the flora and fauna of those remote regions the *Beagle* was to visit. In later life, Darwin maintained that the voyage of the *Beagle* was a major event of his life, for it gave him an opportunity to witness first-hand the many wonders of the natural world and taught him to observe care-fully all that he witnessed. This may be an overstatement; Darwin was already a trained observer of natural phenomena when he left England, and he had accompanied J. S. Henslow, one of the great botanists of the time, on sev-eral collecting expeditions. It was Henslow who recommended Darwin for the post on the *Beagle*, and it may have been the strength of Henslow's rec-ommendation that convinced Captain Fitzroy to accept Darwin. Fitzroy, like many men of his time, judged a man's character by the shape of his facial features, and Fitzroy did not like Darwin's nose.

When he embarked on the *Beagle*, Darwin had not been out of the British Isles, and his experience of human groups, other than those in his native England, was quite limited. Darwin studied medicine briefly in Edin-burgh; he then went to Cambridge where he made the acquaintance of the botanist, Henslow. He accompanied Adam Sedgewick, geology professor, on a walking trip through Wales. At age twenty-two, Darwin had not visited Europe and thus was unfamiliar with other "civilized" cultures, for example, those of the French or Germans, whose lifeways differed from those of the English. Darwin's father and grandfather were physicians, and his childhood was spent in what we would today call an upper middle-class atmosphere. Erasmus Darwin, Charles's grandfather, was a worldly man, but Robert Darwin, Charles's father, appears to have been just the opposite, and Charles was reared in a quiet country life-style. This was the sort of life Darwin chose for himself soon after he returned from his voyage. Most of the people Darwin had seen before his trip were probably much like himself; there was little to challenge his belief that the English way of life was the best possible way of life.

The Darwin family was vehemently opposed to slavery, an ongoing issue in England during Charles's childhood. From 1838, the English began to free slaves in their colonies, starting in the West Indies, and in 1848, the slaves in India were freed. Darwin was certainly exposed to discussions of slavery in his childhood and this may account for his first reaction to it. Loring Brace (personal communication) notes that "The source of Darwin's sensitivity about slavery clearly is derived in part from family traditions. His grandfather, Josiah Wedgewood—his mother's father—was one of the leaders in England's fight against the slave trade, and he developed the very first campaign button which, as produced by his pottery works, was ceramic in its first incarnation."

Under Captain Fitzroy, the *Beagle* sailed from England to the east coast of South America, making many stops to chart that coast, then around the tip of South America, stopping at Tierra del Fuego, up the west coast of South America, and across the Pacific. After stops in Tahiti, New Zealand, and Australia, the *Beagle* sailed across the Indian Ocean, with another stop at Mauritius, then around the southern tip of Africa, and back to Brazil. The *Beagle* returned to England in October, 1836, when Darwin was nearly twenty-seven years old.

Slavery was the first custom that struck him forcibly in Brazil. He recorded in his journal a visit to an estate near Rio de Janeiro. The owner of the estate was contemplating selling the women and children of thirty families, a prospect that appalled Darwin, who wrote:

> I do not believe the inhumanity of separating thirty families, who had lived together for many years, even occurred to the owner. Yet I will pledge myself, that in humanity and good feeling he was superior to the common run of men (*Voyage*:24).

Darwin failed to understand how a *gentleman* could be so inhumane, for such conduct among gentlemen was beyond his experience. He noted that the sale was not made, for reasons of interest and not of humanity, and also observed that he had himself had an uncomfortable encounter with a Negro, who "had been trained to a degradation lower than the slavery of the most helpless animal" (*Voyage*:25). Slavery was a degrading, dehumanizing condition but, as we shall see later, in Darwin's view it had those effects mostly on Negroes.

July 1832 found Darwin on an expedition beyond Maldonado, where he first described the Gauchos. They were "very striking, . . . tall and handsome" but apparently not to be trusted: "their politeness is excessive; they never drink their spirits without expecting you to taste it; but whilst making their exceedingly graceful bow, they seem quite as ready, if occasion offered, to cut your throat" (*Voyage*:43). On this expedition, he encountered unusual customs, and again described them with the precision of a naturalist. On approaching a stranger's house, it was customary to shout "Ave Maria," and then to wait for someone to come out and return the salutation with, "Conceived without sin." Only then was the visitor invited to dismount. Darwin makes no judgment on this custom, but there is a hint of amusement at the silliness of it all.

If gentlemanly conduct in other countries was a disappointment to Darwin, the distinction between Christians and pagans did not fail him and he regularly distinguished between the Christians and the Native Americans. Near Patagonia, he heard of sieges mounted by (indigenous) Araucanians and the maneuvers that had "saved the lives of the Christians." Darwin also described the shooting of thirty-nine Native Americans, as it was told to him by an observer who had witnessed the event. Many of the Patagonians lived nearby, and Darwin saw them himself, noting in his diary that "These Indians are considered civilized; but what their character may have gained by a lesser degree of ferocity, is almost counterbalanced by their entire immorality" (*Voyage*:64). However, in Darwin's eyes, they did possess admirable taste in clothing.

Further inland, while traveling with a group of Gauchos, Darwin spent two days at a ranch where he watched Native American families who came to buy "little articles." The men were tall and fine and the women were sometimes beautiful. Darwin described their division of labor: the men worked at hunting, fighting, and caring for horses; the women loaded and unloaded the horses, made tents, and "in short [were] like the wives of all savages, useful slaves" (*Voyage*:71).

During this trip, Darwin seems to have lost some of his repugnance toward Native Americans, but among a tribe he called "tame," and described as belonging to the Cacique Bernantio, he witnessed events that sickened him: "It was impossible to conceive any thing more wild and savage than the scene of their bivouac. Some drank till they were intoxicated; others swallowed the steaming blood of the cattle slaughtered for their suppers, and then, being sick from drunkenness, they cast it up again, and were besmeared with filth and gore" (*Voyage*:101).

Finally, Darwin mentions the warfare that was going on during his stay, the war between the Native Americans and the European settlers or, in Darwin's terms, the Christians. Those Native Americans who survived were forced to give up their villages and their fishing and take to wandering; Darwin thought it "melancholy" that the Native Americans had given way before the Spanish invaders (*Voyage*:105). He also provided an admiring account of a Native American chief who escaped the slaughter of his people by mounting his horse and hanging on to both the horse and his little son. Darwin notes, "What a fine picture one can form in one's mind—the naked, bronze-like figure of the old man with his little boy, riding like a Mazeppa on the white horse, thus leaving far behind him the host of his pursuers!" (*Voyage*:105).

Traveling inland on the eastern coast of South America, Darwin was the guest of a group of Gauchos who were soldiers in General Rosas's army; Rosas himself was committed to ridding the country of Native Americans, a preoccupation he shared with many settlers. Darwin described Rosas, the governor of Santa Fe, as a tyrant whose government was nonetheless stable and added, "The governor's favourite occupation is hunting Indians: a short time since he slaughtered forty-eight, and sold the children at the rate of three or four pounds apiece" (*Voyage*:129). Massacres of Native American groups were commonplace and Darwin noted, "Shocking is the fact that all the women who appear above twenty years old are massacred in cold blood! When I exclaimed that this appeared rather inhuman, he answered, 'Why, what can be done? they breed so!'" (*Voyage*:103).

The Spanish settlers believed in the rightness of their campaign to exterminate Native Americans, and although Darwin does not seem fully convinced, his protests were mild:

> Everyone here is fully convinced that this is the most just war, because it is against barbarians. Who would believe in this age that such atrocities could be committed in a Christian civilized country? The children of the Indians are saved, . . . as . . . slaves; but I believe in their treatment there is little to complain of (*Voyage*:103).

Darwin predicted that General Rosas would be a good, benevolent ruler; this was the first of several overoptimistic predictions. Rosas became a tyrant, a fact Darwin noted in later editions of the *Voyage*.

Although Darwin never admitted much admiration for the Native Americans he saw, he did develop an admiration for the Gauchos with whom he traveled. Despite his early dismay at the apparent ferocity of the Gauchos, he later included them in the category of "gentlemen," especially as compared with their compatriots. Darwin noted that the Gauchos were superior to the town residents who, though they might be polite, were nonetheless "stained by many vices," including "sensuality, mockery of all religion, and the grossest corruption" (*Voyage*: 157). A year later, he compared the Gauchos with the Guasos of Chile: "The Gaucho, although he may be a cut-throat, is a gentleman; the Guaso is in few respects better, but at the same time a vulgar, ordinary fellow" (*Voyage*:261).

Darwin ended his discourse on his first visit to Spanish South America by thanking the people for their hospitality toward him and praising their good qualities, but although he admired the Gauchos, there is little to indicate that he had gained much respect for the different lifeways that he saw.

It is clear from reading Darwin's journal that he disliked the Spaniards, but his attitude toward Native Americans seems a mixture of pity and disgust. This was a result of his encounter with the Fuegians.

Captain Fitzroy, on an earlier expedition, had taken several Fuegians to England; they were educated at Fitzroy's expense and he cared for them during a lengthy stay. They were on board the *Beagle* bound for home during Darwin's voyage. One of the Fuegians, Jemmy Button, seems to have been a great favorite with the crew and Darwin came to know him. Knowing the Fuegians, however, did little to prepare Darwin for the shock of his first encounter with "savage human beings."

> It was without exception the most curious and interesting spectacle I ever beheld: I could not have believed how wide was the difference between savage and civilized man: it is greater than between a wild and domesticated animal, inasmuch as in man there is a greater power of improvement. . . . Their very attitudes were abject, and the expression of their countenances distrustful, surprised, and startled. After we had presented them with some scarlet cloth, which they immediately tied round their necks, they became good friends. This was shown by the old man patting our breasts, and making a chuckling kind of noise, as people do when feeding chickens. . . . The language of these people, according to our notions, scarcely deserves to be called articulate. Captain Cook has compared it to a man clearing his throat, but certainly no European ever cleared his throat with so many hoarse, guttural and clicking sounds (*Voyage*:205–206).

In his description of Tierra del Fuego and its residents, Darwin uses words like "miserable" and "wretched" quite frequently and most Fuegian activities were described with pejorative adjectives such as "ludicrous" or "foolish." He queried whether these human creatures can be rightly said to enjoy life:

> Viewing such men, one can hardly make oneself believe that they are fellow-creatures, and inhabitants of the same world. It is a common subject of conjecture what pleasure in life some of the lower animals can enjoy: how much more reasonably the same question may be asked with respect to these barbarians! (*Voyage*:213).

Darwin and Fitzroy were misled, probably by the Fuegians on board, into believing that the people of Tierra del Fuego practiced cannibalism, and Darwin observed that there was no reason to believe that the Fuegians had any sort of religious worship, though each group had a wizard or a medicine man. Darwin came away from Tierra del Fuego with a feeling of disgust for the natives; one shipmate had reported seeing a native pick up his child and dash its brains out against the rocks, and Fitzroy's attempt at settling the area with a missionary station was a total failure. Darwin optimistically predicted, in the *Voyage*, that Jemmy Button's children would do a good turn one day for some shipwrecked sailor, but this prediction, like Fitzroy's

mission station, came to naught. In 1859, Jemmy Button himself led a raid-
ing party against a mission station and six missionaries were massacred.

Darwin ended his chapter on Tierra del Fuego on a fairly benign note;
he concluded that the Fuegians existed in a lower state of improvement than
people in other parts of the world but that the Fuegians, as he saw them on
board the *Beagle*, were superior in mental capacity to the Australians of whom
he had read. The Fuegians suffered mightily, Darwin believed, from the "perfect [economic] equality among the individuals composing the Fuegian tribes"
(*Voyage*:230).

Only with the Gauchos did Darwin begin to work through the classic
symptoms of culture shock: he was at first intrigued with the Gauchos and
highly suspicious of them; he spent several weeks among them and learned
something of their way of life, shedding some of his suspicions in the process;
he then incorporated them into his category of "gentlemen." They were better than their countrymen, in Darwin's view, and very nearly in the category
of English gentlemen, Darwin's highest classification.

Had he spent time living with Native Americans, trying to understand
their way of life (as he did those of the animals and birds he studied), Darwin might have arrived at a more accurate assessment of Native Americans;
he might have learned that they indeed had a religion and that they did not
practice cannibalism. But he was content to describe them as wretched and
miserable and to use the Fuegians ever after as the personification of the ignoble savage.

During the rest of the voyage, Darwin saw other Native American
groups; he most often noted their poverty and their mistreatment at the hands
of the Spaniards, but sometimes described their clothing (usually favorably)
and their countenances: "Their expression is generally grave, and even aus-
tere, and possesses much character: this may pass either for honest bluntness
or fierce determination" (*Voyage*:300). Once he expressed mild annoyance
with a Native American guide who "pertinaciously" told him Native American names for every point of the landscape:

> I had with me a guide who knew the country far too well; for he would
> pertinaciously tell me endless Indian names for every little point, rivulet,
> and creek. In the same manner as in Tierra del Fuego, the Indian lan-
> guage appears singularly well adapted for attaching names to the most
> trivial features of the land (*Voyage*:298-299).

He admired the politeness of the Chilenos but was not unhappy when
the *Beagle* sailed away from South America on the last leg of the voyage. In
Tahiti, the ship was met by a party with "laughing, merry faces," and Darwin's belief in facial expressions as indicators of character seemed fully justified by these pleasant (Christian) natives:

> I was pleased with nothing so much as with the inhabitants. There is a
> mildness in the expression of their countenances which at once banishes

the idea of a savage; and an intelligence which shows that they are advancing in civilization (*Voyage*:404).

After eleven days in Tahiti, the *Beagle* continued to New Zealand, whose people were reputed to have been cannibals. Darwin compared the New Zealanders unfavorably with the Tahitians:

> Looking at the New Zealander, one naturally compares him with the Tahitian; both belonging to the same family of mankind. The comparison, however, tells heavily against the New Zealander. He may, perhaps, be superior in energy, but in every other respect his character is of a much lower order. One glance at their respective expressions, brings conviction to the mind that one is a savage, the other a civilized man (*Voyage*:420).

If Darwin did not admire the Maori, the indigenes of New Zealand, neither was he impressed by the emigrant English. This is one of the few times that he says anything unflattering about the English:

> I believe we were all glad to leave New Zealand. It is not a pleasant place. Amongst the natives there is absent that charming simplicity which is found at Tahiti; and the greater part of the English are the very refuse of society (*Voyage*:429).

There was only one "bright spot" in New Zealand—the Christian village of Waimate, in which three large English farmhouses were occupied by three missionary gentlemen. Near these were the native laborers' huts and gardens that produced every fruit and vegetable found in England (*Voyage*:423–424). In Australia, Darwin found another bright spot: Sydney Cove, where the town seemed like an English village, "a most magnificent testimony to the power of the British nation," (*Voyage*:430) and he remarked: "My first feeling was to congratulate myself that I was born an Englishman" (*Voyage*:431). Darwin compared the English colonies with those of the Spanish, and found the latter severely wanting. He was not unaware, however, of the disruptions caused by colonization, and he noted that, "The thoughtless aboriginal, [blinded by peace offerings such as dogs and milk from the settlers] is delighted at the approach of the white man, who seems predestined to inherit the country of his children" (*Voyage*:440). Observing a party of aborigines, Darwin noted that he heard several of their remarks, "which manifested considerable acuteness," and, "On the whole they appear to me to stand some few degrees higher in the scale of civilization than the Fuegians" (*Voyage*:433).

In Australia, Darwin witnessed a native ceremony, a "corrobery," and noted that the natives moved in "hideous harmony" (*Voyage*:449), forming "a perfect display of a festival amongst the lowest barbarians" (*Voyage*:449). The *Beagle* visited Australia and the Pacific in 1836, then returned briefly to Brazil before returning to England. Darwin was beginning to pine for English shores, and devoted little time to the description of human groups in the last pages of *Voyage*, except to describe a Malay ceremony as "a most foolish spectacle" (*Voyage*:457), and to note that a group of convicts from India, seen in Port Louis, Mauritius, was surprisingly noble-looking (*Voyage*:482). In his description of the Malaysian ceremony, he mentioned his thoughts of home: "These scenes of the tropics are in themselves so delicious, that they almost equal those dearer ones at home, to which we are bound by each best feeling of the mind" (*Voyage*:457).

This and other allusions to England indicate Darwin's happiness that the voyage was coming to an end, but the book closes with a review of his vivid impressions, among them a description of his horror at scenes of slavery and a condemnation of the Brazilians, of whom Darwin says, "I bear them no good will—a land also of slavery, and therefore of moral debasement" (*Voyage*:495). Darwin came to terms with his feelings about the Brazilians: he disliked them heartily. His detachment was lost and in its place was repugnance; Darwin had begun his description of other human beings by mentioning one of the first Native Americans he saw as a "good specimen of wild Brazilian youth," but this detachment soon failed him, probably when he witnessed the treatment of Negro slaves in Brazil, and he did not recover it. On the journey, he saw many examples of cruelty among both gentlemen and Native Americans. He could dislike the Brazilians for enslaving Negroes, but it is not certain that he considered the Native Americans he saw as anything more than nearly subhuman members of the species. He may have come to terms with this repugnance by adopting the three-stage evolutionary model (savagery–barbarism–civilization) then common in anthropology, through which he believed all humans had passed; Darwin often reiterated his belief that human beings inherited character traits, and it is possible that he thought his English ancestors had inherited a repugnance to cruelty, that the Fuegians had not yet arrived at that stage.

For every incident of bravery or nobility among Native Americans, Darwin recounts several that illustrate their degradation and foolishness. In his later writings, Darwin passionately opposed vivisection and other cruelties practiced on animals, but he refrained from condemnation of human cruelties to other humans. Perhaps he believed that the missionaries were doing the only kind things possible for the Native Americans, or that Native Americans were doomed to extinction and little could be done about their lot. It is difficult to read Darwin's account without wondering whether he would have reached different conclusions had the countenances of the Fuegians been "laughing and merry," like those of the Tahitians. And, too, one must wonder what the outcome would have been had the *Beagle* stopped in Africa long enough for Darwin to gain an impression of African natives in their homeland.

At the conclusion of the *Voyage*, Darwin restates, "I will not even allude to the many heart-sickening atrocities which I authentically heard of; nor would I have mentioned the above revolting details, had I not met with

several people, so blinded by the constitutional gaiety of the negro, as to speak
of slavery as a tolerable evil" (*Voyage*:497). This last statement has often been
commented on and interpreted as a final slap at Captain Fitzroy, who had
argued with Darwin about the appropriateness of slavery for certain peoples.
Fitzroy "clinched" his argument by asking a group of (presumably Negro)
slaves—in the presence of their owner—whether they were happy as slaves.
Darwin recognized that any answer given under those circumstances would
be worthless, but Fitzroy had taken the slaves' positive response as final proof
of the rightness of slavery. Darwin was not convinced, but neither did he rail
against slavery for Native Americans or other "savages." His final comment
on the human groups he saw on the voyage is again a comparison of the difference between savage and civilized humans; and this comparison comes back
to animals:

> I do not believe it is possible to describe or paint the difference between
> savage and civilized man. It is the difference between a wild and tame
> animal: and part of the interest in beholding a savage, is the same which
> would lead every one to desire to see the lion in his desert, the tiger tear-
> ing his prey in the jungle, or the rhinoceros wandering over the wild
> plains of Africa (*Voyage*:501).

Interest in seeing a savage parallels—but does not exceed—that of seeing a wild animal in its natural habitat. Ever after, Darwin's allusions to savages were filled with or followed immediately by unflattering comparisons to
wild animals, as in tigers tearing their prey.

Had Darwin been just another traveler, his opinions would have been
disregarded long ago. Because he was the founder of the modern evolutionary paradigm, all his opinions were taken seriously, even on subjects on which
he made no pretense to expertise. He was a naturalist and a good observer
of natural phenomena; as an observer of human beings, however, he was
blinded by his own prejudices and prey to his own ethnocentrism. In later
life, he lost his faith in religion but he never changed his opinions about the
"godless" savages he had seen. Darwin revolutionized human thinking about
natural phenomena, but he regularly reiterated xenophobic English ideas
about other human groups and these ideas are still sometimes repeated. For
example, in an outstandingly bad recent novel, Richard Marks (1991, *Three
Men of the Beagle*) uses Darwin's observations as the basis for characterizing
the Yahgan people of Tierra del Fuego:

> The Yahgans had no oral history. They had no myths. They told no
> stories. They had no music or poetry. They had no rituals of any sort, no
> ceremonies, not even for eating, and none for mating. What the Yahgans
> did have was—fire. . . . I think the Americas were peopled by random
> movement of one group and another and another, by spasms of the prim-
> itive mind. This was the dynamic of their nomadism. It was not at all a
> steady or planned movement but a series of irrational twitches that

revealed an underlying restlessness which might lie dormant for a very long time but then would assert itself for no comprehensible reason at a moment no one could have foretold (Marks 1991:15–22).

Although Darwin came to terms with his dislike for the Brazilians, he seldom professed dislike for natives. Instead, he found them immoral or degraded (as he had initially found the Brazilians) and a major task in later works was to explain why the natives were so immoral. These value-laden, judgmental terms and the tones in which the opinions were rendered made it easy for Darwin's readers to believe that if they were to journey to Tierra del Fuego or Australia, they, too, would find immoral and degraded savages with nothing to recommend them.

At the conclusion of his book about the voyage, Darwin says that on balance he would not advise someone to undertake a long circumnavigation of the world, unless that person had a specific interest in a particular branch of knowledge that could be advanced in no other way. For himself, the pleasures had not outweighed the "evils": "No doubt it is a high satisfaction to behold various countries and the many races of mankind, but the pleasures gained at the time do not counterbalance the evils" (*Voyage*:498). Whether Darwin might have planned future voyages is not known; in the event, poor health kept him close to home for the rest of his life.

We do Darwin an injustice by expecting that his views will conform to our own "enlightened" ones, but we do ourselves an injustice by reading into Darwin's opinions our own current ideas about what is humane and just behavior. In the *Descent*, Darwin's reworkings of his early observations are stated so as to lend credence to the nineteenth-century tripartite evolutionary scheme, savagery–barbarism–civilization. Darwin held what we now see as the popular nineteenth-century view of other human groups, popular because it restated English horror, repugnance, and occasional sympathy, for the natives. And who was there to say him nay? The oft-quoted story goes that Sir J. G. Frazer, the great nineteenth-century popularizer of anthropology who wrote many volumes about savages and their beliefs, was once asked if he had ever come into contact with a native. His answer: "but God forbid!" The noble savage of Rousseau and other eighteenth-century philosophers became, in Darwin's observations and evolutionary theories, the ignoble savage whose very humanity had to be explained away in a world striving for perfection.

ALFRED RUSSEL WALLACE AND THE OTHERS

There were few men of stature who could have opposed Darwin's views of other groups, but Alfred Russel Wallace, Darwin's codiscoverer of natural selection, did so. Like Darwin, Wallace traveled extensively to little-known parts of the world, but unlike Darwin, Wallace traveled to earn a livelihood and thus was forced to live among "savages," to rely on them for help with his collecting. As a consequence, Wallace gained considerable respect for the mental abilities of those who lived according to ideas and customs other than English ones. This respect began to manifest itself on his first voyage, to South America. Loren Eiseley has said of Wallace that

> Alone among the great Victorian evolutionists, [Wallace] had actually lived with primitive men. He had not just gazed at them politely from exploring vessels. He had ventured into the high Amazons; he had visited country untrod by Europeans. He had sweated with naked savages up dangerous river portages. He had drunk at their feasts, slept in their houses, observed every aspect of their lives (1979:21).

When he arrived in South America in May of 1848, Wallace was twenty-five years old and a self-described skeptic. He dated the origins of his skepticism to an early influence: "From the age of fourteen I lived with an elder brother, of advanced liberal and philosophical opinions, and I soon lost (and have never since regained) all capacity of being affected in my judgments, either by clerical influence or religious prejudice" (Wallace 1889). In his account of this trip, published as *A Narrative of Travels on the Amazon and Rio Negro, with an Account of the Native Tribes* (hereafter *Narrative*), Wallace noted that previously he had made one short trip to mainland Europe and otherwise had visited only England, so that everything in Brazil had the "charm of perfect novelty." Nevertheless he was disappointed, but he phrased that disappointment in terms very different from those of Darwin:

> The general impression of the city to a person fresh from England is not very favourable. There is such a want of neatness and order, such an appearance of neglect and decay, such evidences of apathy and indolence, as to be at first absolutely painful. But this soon wears off, and some of these peculiarities are seen to be dependent on the climate (*Narrative*:5).

Wallace and the friend with whom he traveled, H. W. Bates, immediately set about learning Portuguese and acclimating themselves to the region, its local customs, and diet. Later, Wallace seems to have learned some of the Indian languages as well, and certainly took great pains to record as much of the languages as he could; these linguistic records were viewed by some critics as a detriment to the first edition of his *Narrative* and were removed from the second edition.

Wallace and Bates lived in the towns for a while, before each went his separate way to collect specimens. Wallace's comparison of Brazilian with English towns is telling:

> Nothing impressed me more than the quiet and orderly state of the city and neighbourhood. No class of people carry knives or other weapons, and there is less noise, fighting, or drunkenness in the streets both day and night, than in any town in England of equal population. When it is remembered that the population is mostly uneducated, that it consists of

slaves, Indians, Brazilians, Portuguese, and foreigners, and that rum is sold at every corner at about twopence per pint, it says much for the good-nature and pacific disposition of the people (*Narrative*:33).

Wallace, then, recorded his impressions of Brazil in terms very different from Darwin's. He also wrote a number of letters from Brazil to Samuel Stevens, a "natural history" agent who used Wallace's letters in his advertising. In one letter, Wallace summarized his views about uncivilized people:

The more I see of uncivilized people, the better I think of human nature, and the essential differences between civilized and savage men seem to disappear (written in 1855, quoted in Wallace 1905:I:368).

In January 1851, he reported to Stevens about time he spent among the Indians and what he hoped to accomplish:

I have been spending a month with some Indians three days' journey up a narrow stream (called the Cobati River). . . .
. . . On my return from there I shall take a voyage up the great river Uapes, and another up the Isanna, not so much for my collections, which I do not expect to be very profitable there, but because I am so much interested in the country and the people that I am determined to see and know more of it and them than any other European traveller. If I do not get profit, I hope at least to get some credit as an industrious and perse-vering traveller (Wallace, quoted in Brooks 1984:27).

In his Amazonian travels, Wallace became interested in the many and varied species of palm trees he saw and, for enlightenment, he turned to the people of the Amazon. In so doing, he did something almost unique for travelers of his century: he took account of the Native American view of species and he records that

During my residence in the Amazon district I took every opportunity of determining the limits of species, and I soon found that the Amazon, the Rio Negro and the Madeira formed the limits beyond which certain species never passed. The native hunters are perfectly acquainted with this fact, and always cross over the river when they want to procure particular animals, which are found even on the river's bank on one side, but never by any chance on the other. . . . (Wallace, quoted in Brooks 1984:35).

Unlike Darwin, who was annoyed by his guide's "pertinacious" insis-tence on describing local words for natural features, Wallace listened carefully to the indigenous terms, recorded them, and sought to elicit their meanings. He ended by describing a new species of palm, *Leopoldina piassaba*, taking the species name from the Native American word, *iassaba*. This is one example of Wallace's way of working and thinking. To understand him more fully and to complete the contrast with Darwin, we must go through his *Narra-tive* more carefully. Wallace does not mention wars of extermination against the Indians at the time he was in Brazil; nor does he seem to have come into contact with high-ranking government officials as often as Darwin apparently did. It seems that Wallace was in the forest collecting specimens more often than Darwin was, and it is certain that he often spent weeks dealing mainly with the local people and the occasional Brazilian colonist.

Like most Englishmen of his time, Wallace probably had not encountered slavery before; seeing it in Brazil caused him to think deeply on the subject, especially after he met Senhor Calistro, a slaveholder whom he described as being "as kind and good-tempered a man as I have ever met with" (*Narrative*:84) and took particular note of Senhor Calistro's excellent treatment of his slaves, "just as he would to a large family of children" (*Narrative*:82–83). After saying he thought that Senhor Calistro's example was perhaps the most favorable example of slavery, he asked:

> But looking at it in this, its most favourable light, can we say that slavery is good or justifiable? Can it be right to keep a number of our fellow-creatures in a state of adult infancy,—of unthinking childhood? It is the responsibility and self-dependence of manhood that calls forth the highest powers and energies of our race. It is the struggle for existence, the "battle of life," which exercises the moral faculties and calls forth the latent sparks of genius. The hope of gain, the love of power, the desire of fame and approbation, excite to noble deeds, and call into action all those faculties which are the distinctive attributes of man (*Narrative*:83).

Wallace's answer was unequivocal:

> And as the teetotalers have declared that the example of the moderate drinker is more pernicious than that of the drunkard, so may the philanthropist consider that a good and kind slave-master does an injury to the cause of freedom, by rendering people generally unable to perceive the false principles inherent in the system, and which, whenever they find a suitable soil in the bad passions of man, are ready to spring up and produce effects so vile and degrading as to make honest men blush for disgraced human nature (*Narrative*:84).

Years later, in his autobiography, Wallace came back to the discussion of slavery, this time coupling it with the issues of Irish self-government and justice. On a visit to America, the question of the Irish arose in discussion and Wallace summarized his thoughts after noting that people who discuss slavery often argue that slaves have to be governed because they are unfit for self-government:

> But to my mind, the question of good or bad, fit or not fit for self-government, is not to the point. It is a question of fundamental justice, and the just is always the expedient, as well as the right. It is a crime against humanity for one nation to govern another *against its will*. The master always says his slaves are not *fit* for freedom; the tyrant, that

subjects are not *fit* to govern themselves. The fitness for self-government is inherent in human nature. Many savage tribes, many barbarian peoples, are really better governed to-day than the majority of the self-styled civilized nations. America deserves the gratitude of all upholders of liberty by founding her own freedom on the principle of immutable *right* to self-government—that Governments derive their just powers only from the consent of the governed. To-day, however, America has taken leave of this high ideal, and has become, like ourselves, a tyrant, ruling the Philippinos against their will as we have so long ruled the Irish (1905:II:121).

On the subject of tame Indians versus those still living in the forest, Wallace had this to say:

I have myself had opportunities of observing the Aborigines of the interior, in places where they retain all their native customs and peculiarities. These truly uncivilised Indians are seen by few travellers, and can only be found by going far beyond the dwellings of white men, and out of the ordinary track of trade. In the neighbourhood of civilisation the Indian loses many of his peculiar customs—changes his mode of life, his house, his costume, and his language—becomes imbued with the prejudices of civilisation, and adopts the forms and ceremonies of the Roman Catholic religion. In this state he is a different being from the true denizen of the forests, and it may be doubted, where his civilisation goes no further than this, if he is not a degenerate and degraded one; but it is in this state alone that he is met with by most travellers in Brazil, on the banks of the Amazon, in Venezuela, and in Peru (*Narrative*:331).

Wallace went on to record his astonishment at seeing "real uncivilised inhabitants" in phrases similar to Darwin's but with very different undertones:

I do not remember a single circumstance in my travels so striking and new, or that so well fulfilled all previous expectations, as my first view of the real uncivilised inhabitants of the river Uapes. Though I had been already three years in the country, and had seen Indians of almost every shade of colour and every degree of civilisation, I felt that I was as much in the midst of something new and startling, as if I had been instantaneously transported to a distant and unknown country (*Narrative*:332).

Once again, unlike Darwin (cited above, *Voyage*:501), who turned immediately to a comparison of wild and tame animals, remarking that the interest in beholding a savage is the same as that which would cause someone to want to see "the tiger tearing his prey in the jungle," Wallace continued with descriptions of houses, villages, clothing, and customs of the Indians that he saw; his observations take the form of a final appendix to the *Narrative*, in which he records as much as he can about the differences and similarities between the Native American groups he saw and was told about.

Darwin believed in the civilizing power of property, and did not see much hope for the progress of "savage" tribes until they had artificial governments:

> The perfect equality among the individuals composing the Fuegian tribes, must for a long time retard their civilization. As we see those animals, whose instinct compels them to live in society and obey a chief, are most capable of improvement, so is it with the races of mankind. Whether we look at it as a cause or a consequence, the more civilized always have the most artificial governments. For instance, the inhabitants of Otaheite, who, when first discovered, were governed by hereditary kings, had arrived at a far higher grade than another branch of the same people, the New Zealanders,—who, although benefited by being compelled to turn their attention to agriculture, were republicans in the most absolute sense. In Tierra del Fuego, until some chief shall arise with power sufficient to secure any acquired advantage, such as the domesticated animals, it seems scarcely possible that the political state of the country can be improved. At present, even a piece of cloth given to one is torn into shreds and distributed; and no one individual becomes richer than another. On the other hand, it is difficult to understand how a chief can arise till there is property of some sort by which he might manifest his superiority and increase his power. . . . (*Voyage*:230–231).

In contrast to Darwin's suggestion that the problems with savage society resulted from their "perfect equality," Wallace looked at the customary division of labor, and remarked:

> These people almost always seem at work, but have very little to show for it. . . . This is principally the result of everybody doing everything for himself, slowly and with much unnecessary labour, instead of occupying himself with one kind of industry, and exchanging his produce for the articles he requires. An Indian spends a week in cutting down a tree in the forest, and fashioning an article which, by the division of labour, can be made for sixpence: the consequence is, that his work produces but sixpence a week, and he is therefore all his life earning a scanty supply of clothing, in a country where food may be had almost for nothing (*Narrative*:118).

Another aspect of Darwin's ideas about other people or groups is that he records almost nothing that is good *and* bad about the people he met with. Except for the Gauchos, who were "cutthroat gentlemen," the natives are either good or bad, seldom a combination, nor is the other side usually alluded to in Darwin's writings. Wallace, however, suggests there were two sides to every story: he tells of kindhearted Brazilians having their homes and property destroyed by Indians, and of Indian women mistreated by their Brazilian lovers. Wallace, too, ended up not liking the Brazilians, but he sought to understand their circumstances:

On the subjects of the most prevalent kinds of immorality, it is impossible to enter, without mentioning facts too disgusting to be committed to paper. Vices of such a description as at home are never even alluded to, are here the subjects of common conversation, and boasted of as meritorious acts, and no opportunity is lost of putting the vilest construction upon every word or act of a neighbour.

Among the causes which tend to promote the growth of such widespread immorality, we may perhaps reckon the geographical position and political condition of the country, and the peculiar state of civilisation in which it now exists (*Narrative*:264).

Later in his life, Wallace made several voyages to other parts of the world, particularly to Malaya, New Guinea, and Borneo. These voyages, he says, were motivated by his interest in the species problem, and by his need to finance his studies by collecting specimens for sale. It was on one of these trips that he had the insight that caused him to write to Darwin—who was by then a well-established naturalist—about his thoughts on the workings of natural selection.

Although Wallace does not mention the emotions that would indicate he was passing through culture shock, he came out of Brazil with more thoughtful appraisals than Darwin did, and the quality of those appraisals suggests that he had indeed become a cultural relativist, though by no means one who believed that the "natives" were always right. But the implications of these contrasts should be clear: Darwin never had to live with the "savages" for whom he had so little sympathy, whereas Wallace, who did have to live with indigenous peoples, hunt with them, and attempt to learn their languages and customs, gained a good deal of respect for other peoples, other lifeways. Darwin seems never to have gone all the way through the various phases of culture shock, whereas Wallace did so and came out a cultural relativist, long before the term was invented.

Wallace ends his *Narrative* not, as Darwin did, by warning off prospective travelers but by voicing his regrets that his notes and specimens were lost when his ship caught fire on the return voyage. Later, however, a clue to his thinking about prospective travelers may be found in his record of an encounter with a Russian anthropologist introduced to him by Darwin's friend, Thomas Henry Huxley; the anthropologist planned to spend several months in New Guinea. Wallace says:

One of those occasions that I particularly remember was to meet Dr. Miklucho Maklay, a Russian anthropologist, who was going to New Guinea, and as I was the only Englishman who had lived some months alone in that country, Huxley thought we should be interested with each other.

Maklay's . . . idea was that you could really learn nothing about natives unless you lived with them and became almost one of themselves; above all, you must win their confidence, and must therefore begin by trusting them absolutely. . . . This was, I think, in the winter of 1870–71. Both Huxley and myself thought this plan exceedingly risky, but he determined to try it; and he succeeded, but through the exercise of an amount of coolness and courage which very few men indeed possess. . . .

[The doctor] lived with these people for fifteen months, learnt their language, studied them minutely, and explored much of the surrounding country. I know of no more daring feat by any traveller (1905, II:34–36).

Darwin never fully embraced the idea of biological determinism (the notion that biology determined one's abilities). Although he vacillated on this question with respect to human races, he seems to have been quite certain that it did apply to the differences between men and women when he wrote:

Man is more courageous, pugnacious and energetic than woman, and has more inventive genius. His brain is absolutely larger, but whether or not proportionately to his larger body, has not, I believe, been fully ascertained" (*Descent*:568–569).

It is generally admitted that with woman the powers of intuition, of rapid perception, and perhaps of imitation, are more strongly marked than in man; but some, at least, of these faculties are characteristic of the lower races, and therefore of a past and lower state of civilisation.

The chief distinction in the intellectual powers of the two sexes is shewn by man's attaining to a higher eminence, in whatever he takes up, than can woman—whether requiring deep thought, reason, or imagination, or merely the uses of the senses and hands. If two lists were made of the most eminent men and women in poetry, painting, sculpture, music (inclusive both of composition and performance), history, science, and philosophy, with half-a-dozen names under each subject, the two lists would not bear comparison. We may also infer, from the law of the deviation from averages, so well illustrated by Mr. Galton, in his work on "Hereditary Genius," that if men are capable of a decided pre-eminence over woman in many subjects, the average of mental power in man must be above that of woman (*Descent*:576).

Wallace believed that women had been denied the opportunity of achievement but that they would come into their own, when education and other opportunities were freely available to them:

The position of women in the not distant future will be far higher and more important than any which has been claimed for or by her in the past.

While she will be conceded full political and social rights on an equality with men, she will be placed in a position of responsibility and power which will render her his superior, since the future moral progress of the race will so largely depend upon her free choice in marriage. As time goes on, and she acquires more and more economic independence, *that* alone will give her an effective choice which she has never had before. But this choice will be further strengthened by the fact that, with ever-increasing approach to equality of opportunity for every child born in our country, that terrible excess of male deaths, in boyhood and early manhood especially due to various preventable causes, will disappear, and change the present majority of women to a majority of men. This will lead to a greater rivalry for wives, and will give to women the power of rejecting all the lower types of character among their suitors.

It will be their special duty so to mould public opinion, through home training and social influence, as to render the women of the future the regenerators of the entire human race (quoted in Osborn 1928:94–95).

So, too, with the question of colonization. Wallace's views on coloniza-tion and the problems it brought were quoted earlier, in the passage con-cerning the extreme immorality of the Brazilians. Darwin's views, as might be expected, were very different, and he congratulated the English on their success as colonists:

The remarkable success of the English as colonists, compared to other European nations, has been ascribed to their "daring and persistent energy;" a result which is well illustrated by comparing the progress of the Canadians of English and French extraction; but who can say how the English gained their energy? There is apparently much truth in the belief that the wonderful progress of the United States, as well as the character of the people, are the results of natural selection; for the more energetic, restless and courageous men from all parts of Europe have emigrated during the last ten or twelve generations to that great country, and have there succeeded best (*Descent*:144).

Darwin also believed that the lack of fertility shown among "savages" might have biological origins.

Seeing how general is this law of the susceptibility of the reproductive system to changed conditions of life, and that it holds good with our nearest allies, the Quadrumana, I can hardly doubt that it applies to man in his primeval state. Hence if savages of any race are induced suddenly to change their habits of life, they become more or less sterile, and their young offspring suffer in health, in the same manner and from the same cause, as do the elephant and hunting-leopard in India, many monkeys in America, and a host of animals of all kinds, on removal from their natural conditions.

We can see why it is that aborigines, who have long inhabited islands, and who must have been long exposed to nearly uniform conditions, should be specially affected by any change in their habits, as seems to be the case. Civilised races can certainly resist changes of all kinds far better than savages; and in this respect they resemble domesticated animals, for though the latter sometimes suffer in health (for instance European dogs in India), yet they are rarely rendered sterile. . . . The immunity of civilised races and domesticated animals is probably due to their having formerly immigrated or being carried from country to country, and to different families or subraces having inter-crossed. It appears that a cross with civilised races at once gives to an aboriginal race an immunity from the evil consequences of changed conditions (*Descent*:194–195).

In this passage there is not one word about the wars of extermination that were conducted against Indians or aborigines in many parts of the world, nor is there any discussion of the devastating diseases Europeans brought. Wallace discussed both these topics in his writings and was aware that disease and warfare were major factors in causing indigenous peoples to be perceived by travelers as inferior specimens of humanity.

These contrasts between Darwin and Wallace could be extended indefinitely. Two anthropologists who have studied Darwin's ideas closely are George W. Stocking, Jr. (1968) and Alexander Alland, Jr. (1985). From what is essentially the same data, they reached very different conclusions. Stocking, in his sixth chapter, "The Dark-Skinned Savage: The Image of Primitive Man in Evolutionary Anthropology" (1968:110–132), suggests that Darwin drew on the (racist, ethnocentric) social evolutionary theories current in anthropology at the time and that he was particularly influenced by Herbert Spencer (1968:113).

In 1985, Alexander Alland published a selection of Darwin's writings on humans from his *Journal*, *The Descent of Man*, and *The Expression of Emotions in Man and the Animals*. Alland quotes Stephen Jay Gould's (1982) suggestions that although Darwin was an abolitionist, he was not an egalitarian; and that although Darwin was not a racist, neither was he a relativist (Alland 1985:10). Alland believes that Darwin was least racist when he was forming his opinions on the basis of real encounters he experienced but that he was led astray by his reading of anthropological sources.

There is disagreement, too, on what kind of observer Darwin was: James Boon (1982:42) quotes Darwin on Patagonian "giants" and suggests that he was a poor observer. I agree with Alland (1985) that Darwin was by no means a poor observer, but I believe that Darwin was misled when it came to humans both by his own cultural preconceptions and by his reading of the anthropological literature.

Whatever the interpretation given to the differences between the two men, it is certain that Wallace admired Darwin. Some passages in Wallace's *Narrative* sound as if they were constructed with Darwin's *Voyage* as model, but Wallace arrived at very different conclusions and we must wonder why. One answer may have had to do with religious convictions: as noted, Wallace was a skeptic from an early age, whereas Darwin set off on his voyage just before he was to become a vicar. Later in their lives, both Darwin and

Wallace eschewed the formal religion of their childhood for different reasons and with very different outcomes. Wallace's nonconformist views took him from skepticism to spiritualism and led him on to conclusions that were unacceptable to leading scientists and thinkers of his day: he opposed vaccination, favored Irish land reform, championed the rights of women, and so on. More important, his logic led him to conclusions unacceptable to Darwin. Wallace vacillated between extreme racist views about the inferiority of other cultures (1864) and a relativist view based on what he had seen of human beings in "primitive" cultures, and finally he arrived at a conclusion disliked by the Darwinian materialists: human evolution was guided by a Divine Hand, which had overseen the evolution of human beings and caused them—universally—to be in possession of mental faculties beyond those necessary for survival. Wallace ended his days hearing "celestial music of the spheres" and being avoided by most of his peers; Darwin helped to secure a pension for him so that he was not completely destitute. We cannot know what the outcomes might have been if the distinction between race and culture had been firmly embedded in the science of the times and if Wallace had been the sole discoverer of natural selection as the mechanism of evolution.

What we do know is that the science of Darwin's time, like Darwin himself, grappled unsuccessfully with the distinction between race and culture, perhaps because of Darwin's ethnocentrism and that of his scientific colleagues. We also see that anthropological fieldwork, as it is now practiced, has led most anthropologists to ideas closer to those of Wallace than of Darwin. Apart from Eiseley (1961), however, few anthropologists have noted that Wallace was an outstanding model for anthropology and its current methods. Eiseley remarked that "It is interesting to observe that Wallace reveals scarcely a trace of the racial superiority so frequently manifested in nineteenth-century scientific circles" (1961:303). It is even more interesting that Darwin's (often recounted) views and Wallace's (usually ignored) ideas have not been subjected to serious critique by those concerned with the beginnings of ethnographic understandings and the ongoing revisions of those understandings characteristic of this decade (Boon 1982; Clifford 1988; Marcus and Fischer 1986; Shanklin in preparation). Wallace had opinions on almost every subject and some of them we now find quirky or bizarre, such as his fierce opposition to vaccination. It is more surprising, perhaps, that in the course of the last century, anthropological opinions have swung from Darwin's view of other human groups to Wallace's. The comparison of Darwin and Wallace points up the need for an interesting book, yet to be written, about changes in ideas over time and the length of time that an idea, scientifically advanced, takes to fully enter the popular consciousness and be accepted. In a few centuries, the Western world has moved from flat earth to round planet conceptions, from heliocentric to solarcentric theories; how much longer will it take to move from folk taxonomies of race to an understanding of human diversity?

DISCUSSION QUESTIONS

1. Compare your own travel experiences or other situations in which you came into contact with "Others" whose ideas were very different from yours. How did you handle the situation? Would you do it the same way again? Why or why not?

2. Have you ever had culture shock? Some people who haven't traveled very much experience "life shock," not culture shock, when they meet people whose expectations are very different from their own; for example, when they go from a small high school to a large university or when they move from one coast to another. Has this happened to you? What were your reactions?

FURTHER READING

Both Darwin and Wallace are well worth reading, although some of Darwin's writings can be rough going. The two books featured in this and the next chapter, Darwin's *Voyage* and Wallace's *Narrative,* however, are very clear and can be highly recommended. A delightful book about Darwin's journey is Alan Moorehead's *Darwin and the Beagle* (New York: Harper & Row, 1969). Darwin's own autobiography also makes engaging (if not entirely factual) reading: *The Autobiography of Charles Darwin: 1809–1882,* edited by Nora Barlow (New York: W. W. Norton, 1958). Recently, Darwin himself has become the subject of a whole industry devoted to understanding every aspect of his life, and the biographies available are written from very different viewpoints.

An interesting recent book on the concept of culture shock is *On Being Foreign: Culture Shock in Short Fiction,* edited by Tom J. Lewis and Robert E. Jungman (Yarmouth, ME: Intercultural Press, 1986).

Darwin, Charles 1962 [1860] *The Voyage of the Beagle.* Garden City, NY: Anchor Books.

Wallace, Alfred Russel 1969 [1853] *A Narrative of Travels on the Amazon and Rio Negro, with an Account of the Native Tribes.* New York: Haskell House.

Wallace has not been written about recently (but see Fichman, below), whereas Darwin has been the subject of innumerable new biographies and commentaries. Among the best are:

Biographies

Bowlby, John 1990 *Charles Darwin: A New Life.* New York: W. W. Norton. Focuses on Darwin's early loss of his mother as the root cause of his illnesses later in life.

Darwin, Francis 1898 *The Life and Letters of Charles Darwin.* 2 vols. New York: D. Appleton. This compilation by Darwin's son contains a number of useful insights.

Desmond, Adrian, and James Moore 1992 *Darwin*. New York: Warner Books.
The authors' hope is to reveal all possible aspects of Darwin's day-to-day life and thought, as well as to portray him as a man of his time.

Fichman, Martin 1981 *Alfred Russel Wallace*. Boston: Twayne.
A somewhat critical biography with a fine discussion of Wallace's shifts in attitudes and ideas.

George, Wilma 1964 *Biologist Philosopher: A Study of the Life and Writings of Alfred Russel Wallace*. London: Abelard-Schuman.

Himmelfarb, Gertrude 1959 *Darwin and the Darwinian Revolution*. London: Chatto and Windus.
A historian's view.

Marchant, James 1975 [1916] *Alfred Russel Wallace: Letters and Reminiscences*. New York: Arno Press.

McKinney, H. Lewis 1972 *Wallace and Natural Selection*. New Haven: Yale University Press.

Commentaries and Comparisons

Barrett, Paul H., and Howard E. Gruber 1980 *Metaphysics, Materialism and the Evolution of Mind: Early Writings of Charles Darwin*. Chicago: University of Chicago Press.
Mainly concerned with the title subject matter but contains some interesting thoughts about Darwin's embrace of the inheritance of mental characteristics.

Bowler, Peter J. 1988 *The Non-Darwinian Revolution: Reinterpreting a Historical Myth*. Baltimore: Johns Hopkins University Press.

Brackman, Arnold C. 1980 *A Delicate Arrangement: The Strange Case of Charles Darwin and Alfred Russel Wallace*. New York: Times Books.
The author believes that Darwin and several friends conspired to secure priority and credit for the idea of natural selection for Darwin.

Cronin, Helena 1992 *The Ant and the Peacock: Altruism and Sexual Selection from Darwin to Today*. New York: Cambridge University Press.

Durant, John R. 1979 Scientific Naturalism and Social Reform in the Thought of Alfred Russel Wallace. *British Journal for the History of Science* 12:33–35.

Glick, Thomas F., ed. 1980 *The Comparative Reception of Darwinism*. Austin: University of Texas Press.
Interesting collection of articles on the impact of Darwinism on European and American societies.

Gould, Stephen Jay 1980a Natural Selection and the Human Brain: Darwin *vs.* Wallace. In *The Panda's Thumb*. Pp. 47–59. New York: W. W. Norton.

1980b Wallace's Fatal Flaw. *Natural History* 89(1):26–40.

Gruber, Howard E. 1981 *Darwin on Man: A Psychological Study of Scientific Creativity*. 2nd edition. Chicago: University of Chicago Press.

Kohn, David, ed. 1985 *The Darwinian Heritage*. Princeton: Princeton University
    Press.
    This collection contains some excellent articles on the subjects mentioned here,
    including Frank J. Sullaway's content analysis of Darwin's letters to J. S. Henslow,
    written while Darwin was aboard the *Beagle*, in "Darwin's Early Intellectual
    Development: An Overview of the *Beagle* Voyage"; John R. Durant's discussion
    of the primacy Darwin gave to anthropomorphism (versus anthropocentrism) in
    "The Ascent of Nature in Darwin's *Descent of Man*"; and Malcolm Jay Kottler's
    careful comparison of Darwin's and Wallace's positions on the origins of sterility
    and sexual dimorphism and their disagreements about the human brain, in
    "Charles Darwin and Alfred Russel Wallace: Two Decades of Debate Over
    Natural Selection."

Kottler, Malcolm J. 1974 Alfred Russel Wallace, the Origin of Man, and Spiritualism.
    Isis 65:174–180.

4

●

Race, Culture, and Eugenics

In the previous chapter, I contrasted the ideas of Charles Darwin and Alfred Russel Wallace about human beings and their innate abilities and noted that the answer to Wallace's dilemma was in the concept of culture, the idea of learned abilities available to all humans at whatever level of technology. But this answer was not to be fully accepted in anthropology until the middle of the twentieth century, after race was discarded as a scientific concept. In the meantime, the notion of what constituted a race had undergone some important changes. Before looking at the split between race and culture as anthropological concepts, it is worthwhile to review the phases through which the race concept passed before being discarded by anthropologists. I will summarize its history in anthropology in three phases, which are not mutually exclusive:

1. Race as a *conglomerate descriptive* term, before anthropology came into being (Linnaean, pre-Darwinian, and Darwinian, seventeenth and eighteenth centuries)

2. Race as a *typological device* (Darwinian, largely nineteenth century) in combination with some Darwinian evolutionary notions

3. Race refined as a category within what is sometimes called the *modern synthetic theory* (the blending of Darwinian theory with genetic theory, twentieth century) and its ultimate replacement by the idea of breeding populations and their adaptation to specific environments (Bleibtreu and Meaney 1973:224).

The question, why are there differences among human groups? is now asked and answered very differently by physical anthropologists. Typologies and inferior/superior rankings no longer enter into the discussions, and very small differences, such as vitamin D absorption or sickling genes, are studied for their adaptive significance within particular environments. And, too, physical anthropologists talk about differences between and within groups, the study of human physical variations. They "believe" not in the existence of races but in populations, usually studied as breeding populations that have a number of physical (not cultural or mental) characteristics in common, such as blood type or eye color.

There are other ways of dividing up these phases. Banton (1987) has described a three-phase view of racial thought in slightly different terms: first, from the sixteenth to the nineteenth century, race as lineage, groups connected by common descent; second, in the early nineteenth century, race as type, as a limited number of permanent forms; and third, after Darwin, in the mid-nineteenth century, race as subspecies (1987:xi).

Nancy Stepan (1982) also divides the phases differently: first, she sees as the "pre-modern" period the time between 1600 and 1800, when involvement in the slave trade and the growth of ethnocentrism contributed to definitions of other races as inferior; second, the modern period between 1800 and 1960 when scientific credence was lent to the notions of racial inferiority and superiority; and third, from 1960 onward, the time when race was discarded by the scientific community as a device for classifying human beings.

Stepan regards the period between 1860 and 1900 as the "heyday of Darwinism" and suggests that the embrace of Darwinism "was compatible with the idea of the fixity, antiquity, and hierarchy of human races" (1982:49). Evolution was used to lend strength to ideas about the superiority of white races, the inferiority of dark races, and eventually, to the cause of the eugenicists. Richard Hofstadter observed that "in some respects the United States during the last three decades of the nineteenth and at the beginning of the twentieth century was *the* Darwinian country. England gave Darwin to the world, but the United States gave to Darwinism an unusually quick and sympathetic reception" (Hofstadter 1955:4–5).

Stocking (1968:115) refers to this period at the end of the nineteenth century as a Darwinian "milieu" in which

> Darwinian evolution, evolutionary ethnology, and polygenist race thus interacted to support a raciocultural hierarchy in terms of which civilized men, the highest product of social evolution, were large-brained white men, and only large-brained white men, the highest products of organic evolution, were civilized. The assumption of white superiority was certainly not original with Victorian evolutionists; yet the interrelation of the theories of cultural and organic evolution, with their implicit hierarchy of race, gave it a new rationale (1968:122).

Banton notes that in response to the question, "'Why are they not like us', the typologists answered, 'Because they have always been different'" (1987:64). Within the typological framework, there was another vexatious question: how long "they" had been different or the general question of the origin of the human species. Those who argued for a single origin were called monogenists, referring to the belief that all humans were descended from one original "Adam and Eve," and those who argued for multiple origins were polygenists, who thought that humans had had separate origins on different continents. Johann F. Blumenbach, Samuel Stanhope Smith (said by Ashley Montagu to be the first American anthropologist), Charles Darwin, Thomas Henry Huxley, and Alfred Russel Wallace were monogenists; Samuel George Morton, Paul Broca, and William Z. Ripley were polygenists.

Franz Boas, a monogenist, and the group of anthropology students he trained took for granted that all human beings learned their ways of behaving, that behavior was not inherent; the eugenics school believed the opposite, that people's behavior was tied to their genetic makeup and could not be changed. The answer Boasian anthropology gave to the question of why there were differences was that differences were primarily a matter of environment and learning, with perhaps some unknown influences of heredity. Here I contrast Boas's ideas about the plasticity of human abilities and physical characteristics with two very different ideas: first, nineteenth-century notions known as "typological" theories, having to do with the fixity of human behavior and, second, the need for improving racial stocks, as formulated in the American school of eugenics in the early decades of the twentieth century.

RACE AS A CONGLOMERATE, DESCRIPTIVE DEVICE

Scientists are uncertain about the origins of the word *race*, but some believe that it might have come originally from an Arabic word, *ras*, which means head or beginning (Boyd 1950). From the Arabic, the word went into Spanish or Italian, and the fourteenth-century Spanish word, *raza*, means kind or sort, a kind or sort of animal, for example (*Webster's New World Dictionary*: *razza*, Italian; *ratio*, Latin). Before the mid-nineteenth century the word *race* was used in much the same way we might now use the words *strain* or *variety*. Writers spoke in terms of a "race of kings" or a "race of yeomen" (Curtis 1968); John Bunyan in the seventeenth century wrote about a "race of saints" (quoted in Banton and Harwood 1975:13).

The conglomerate descriptive use was "formalized" by Linnaeus, who first published his classifications in 1735 but referred only to *Homo sapiens* (literally, wise man), and did not distinguish the species according to races or varieties in the first edition. In a subsequent (1738) edition of his catalog, Linnaeus added the four "varieties" of *Homo sapiens*: *americanus*; *europaeus*; *asiaticus*;

and *aser*. Europeans were "light, lively and inventive," whereas the American Indians (*H. s. americanus*) were "choleric and persevering" (Count 1950:357). The Asiatics (*H. s. asiaticus*) were "yellow, melancholic, inflexible"; and the Africans (*H. s. aser*) were "phlegmatic, indulgent, crafty, lazy and negligent" (Count 1950:357).

These four varieties were essentially geographical classifications; although Linnaeus noted certain temperamental characteristics that went along with the varieties, the divisions were based on the four major geographical divisions of the earth—Europe, Asia, Africa, and the Americas—along with the skin colors found in the human species in each place. As we have seen, early explorers, Herodotus among them, had also noted the differences and speculated that they were due to the environment. Later explorers offered similar speculations and as we have seen, Charles Darwin used facial expressions to judge the cultural characteristics of other groups.

Geography and skin color differences were the main diagnostics—there were yellow people in Asia, white people in Europe, black people in Africa, and red people in America. In the conglomerate descriptive use of race, other characteristics, such as mental or cultural traits, were often mingled with physical attributes; in contemporary terms, this made it a racist scheme because it mixed physical and cultural characteristics. Linnaeus's scientific intent was to classify, not to justify racist social policies, but whatever its difficulties, there were theorists of race who wished for a more scientific set of criteria, one that defined only physical traits. It is a truism of the scientific enterprise that the more closely you look at something, the more complicated it becomes. Broad geographical classifications of race were not useful for scientific purposes; to state that skin color varies from one continent to another is not to explain differences but to state the obvious. The many descriptions of skin color variations according to geographic region made it clear that skin color varied, even within a group or within broad continental boundaries; at the edges of the continents, skin color was even more varied, and it became apparent to the classifiers that skin color was not a reliable indicator of race.

Later investigators used skin color more systematically and without the personality characteristics the earlier students of human races had ascribed, but the divisions they saw and the concepts they used quickly became unwieldy. However, the conglomerate descriptive use of race continued well into the twentieth century. In 1946, Earnest Hooton (who later studied the physical anthropology of Ireland) offered a different, somewhat dizzying set of categories: there were primary races such as Whites, Negroids, and Mongoloids. Within each primary race there were primary subraces; among whites there were Mediterranean, Ainu, Keltic, Nordic, and Alpine or East Baltic. Further, there were composite races like the Australian, Indo-Dravidian, and Polynesian. There were also composite subraces such as Armenoid and Dinaric, as well as residual mixed types like the Nordic-Alpine and Nordic-Mediterranean. These divisions usually included additional genetically determined traits.

As late as 1965, Stanley Garn used a conglomerate description when he offered the idea of geographical races: "a collection of race populations, separated from other such collections by major geographical barriers" (1965:14). Among these geographical races were Amerindian, Polynesian, Micronesian, Melanesian-papuan, Australian, Asiatic, Indian, European, and African.

In addition to geographical races, Garn found, there were local races: a breeding population adapted to local selection pressures and maintained by either natural or social barriers to gene interchange (1965:16). Local races included: Northwest European, Northeast European, Alpine, Mediterranean, East African, Bantu, Tibetan, North Chinese, Extreme Mongoloid, and Hindu.

There was another category, too, the microrace, that deserves mention only because it is an indication of just how overelaborate the categories came to be. The term *microrace* was never well defined, but it referred to neighborhoods within a city or to a city itself because "marriage or mating, is a mathematical function of distance. With millions of potential mates, the male ordinarily chooses one near at hand" (Garn 1971:19). Garn gives no examples of these microraces, but Darlington provides an example of a microrace that illustrates both the problems with elaborating categories and the silliness of such categories:

> In all advanced societies crime takes two forms. One is sporadic and
> unorganized. Of this kind was the momentary blaze of shooting which
> killed, . . . some 20,000 men in the western states between 1870 and
> 1895. . . . The second kind is organized, disciplined and professional.
> And insofar as it succeeds it is self-perpetuating and hereditary. . . . [The
> Sicilian Mafia] maintained themselves by blackmail and assassination and
> by enforcing a strict code of honour within their true-breeding society.
>   The first *Mafiosi* arrived in New Orleans in 1890. There, eleven of
> them, imprisoned for murder, were lynched by the kinsmen of their
> victims. The U.S. government . . . innocently agreed to pay $30,000
> compensation for this act of justice. So it began. . . . Selecting their
> recruits exclusively among Sicilian immigrants, they trained them by the
> discipline of the gun and increased them by regular inbreeding in the
> stratified ranks of the hierarchy. . . .
>   The most illustrious families of *cosa nostra* were now joined in marital
> alliances of the same character, although for such a different purpose, as
> the old Philadelphia Quakers and the European royal dynasties with
> which we are familiar. Nothing on earth will make them come to terms
> with the general body of society. They are a race apart (Darlington
> 1969:610–611).

This quotation contains catchphrases that suggest scientific writing about race: hereditary, true-breeding, regular inbreeding, a race apart, and so on. But the reader has to stop to think what is being described: a group only a few decades old with a regional background and some occupational habits in common. Might we also speak of a race of electricians or college professors or auto workers? These are not races, nor is Darlington's a scientific description in any sense, although the use of the term *microrace* suggests that it is. This kind of writing, however, does illustrate a more general point, to do with the endless elaboration of categories and their ultimately ludicrous uses.

RACE AS A TYPOLOGICAL DEVICE

A key concept of the nineteenth century was "typology," a classificatory system according to which races could be systematically grouped because each had "immutable" or unchanging characteristics. Typological notions were pre-Darwinian, but the school reached its zenith when the typological notions were melded with Darwinian emphasis on evolution's conservative forces. The explanation that was given for racial differences was that variations in constitution and behavior were the expression of differences between types that were relatively permanent, that social categories were aligned with the natural categories, and that individuals belonging to a particular racial group displayed an innate antagonism toward other types (Banton 1987:38).

In this phase, there was an attempt to formalize the race concept even further, based on typologies or the study of ideal types and their variant forms. At the turn of the century, Mendel's findings on inheritance were rediscovered and the search for "racial markers" was ended, as heredity was seen to be an important component of physical makeup, but only one component among many others, including environment and culture.

In the beginning, the investigation of racial differences according to typological notions was a productive enterprise, in the sense that the investigations yielded a great deal of data. The differences between human groups could be and were quantified; such traits as nose form, blood groups, eye color, head shape, and skin color were carefully counted and recorded. As time went on, more counts were done and then it seemed still more counts were in order, so investigators were kept busy for years with new counts. The refinement of the measuring tools, the endless elaborations of measurements, and of the classifications that grew out of them, would lead finally to the recognition that diversity was as important as the stability the classifiers initially emphasized. But this was not to happen until typological notions had been employed extensively and exhaustively.

Stephen Jay Gould, in *The Mismeasure of Man*, has gone through the data of several of the leading scientists of the nineteenth century, including Samuel Morton and Paul Broca. Samuel George Morton died in 1851, eight years before Darwin's *Origin of Species* was first published. Morton believed that races could be ranked objectively by measuring the physical characteristics of the brain, and he assembled the largest collection of skulls available in his time. He began his ranking of races by filling the cranial cavity of the skulls with mustard seed, which he poured into the skull and then back into a cylinder marked to give volume in cubic inches. But the mustard seed measurements proved inconsistent, so he switched to lead shot (BBs), which gave more consistent results. Morton's results were those desired: "whites on top, Indians in the middle, and blacks on the bottom" (Gould 1981:53–54). Among Morton's Modern Caucasian Group, Teutons had a mean cranial capacity of 92, those of the Celtic Family had a mean of 87, and those of the Semitic Family a mean of 89. In his American Group, the Toltecan Family, including Incas and Mexicans, had a mean of 79, and his Negro Group a mean of 83 (Gould 1981:55).

But Morton calculated his high Caucasian mean by eliminating small-brained Hindus from his sample (Gould 1981:60) and increasing the number of small-brained Incas; he also failed to remeasure with BBs those skulls that previously had been satisfactorily low. He did these things "baldly," as Gould says, reporting what he had done and justifying it by adding or subtracting groups according to his own (and presumably his readers') expectations. Gould recalculated Morton's rankings and found

> My correction of Morton's conventional ranking reveals *no* significant differences among races for Morton's own data. All groups rank between 83 and 87 cubic inches, and Caucasians share the pinnacle (Gould 1981:67).

Gould does not suggest that Morton intended fraud or conscious manipulation; rather, he says, "All I can discern is an *a priori* conviction about racial ranking so powerful that it directed his tabulations along preestablished lines" (Gould 1981:69).

Paul Broca was a French professor of clinical surgery; he founded the Anthropological Society of Paris in 1859, and like Morton, he believed that intelligence could be assessed by brain or skull measurements. Unlike Morton, Broca did not manipulate his measurements; instead he "explained" them. In 1862, Broca published his "demonstration" that the brain size of Europeans had increased in size over the last centuries' progression from medieval to modern times. He obtained samples from three Parisian cemeteries, from the twelfth, eighteenth, and nineteenth centuries. Initially, the average cranial capacities were a disappointment—1,426, 1,409, and 1,462 cc.— but Broca recovered by introducing the factor of social class. The large twelfth-century sample, obtained in a churchyard, had to represent gentry, whereas the (smaller) eighteenth-century skulls came from a common grave. The nineteenth-century sample came from both individual graves (average 1,484 cc.) and a common grave (1,403 cc.). But the eighteenth-century common grave had a larger average (1,409 cc.) than the nineteenth-century's (1,403 cc.), and Broca explained this by arguing that the eighteenth-century common grave had included a better class of people. In the same way, he resolved another problem, an additional seventeen skulls from the morgue's graveyard, skulls that had a higher value than those from the individual graves of the nineteenth century (1,517 cc. vs. 1,484 cc.). This, Broca said, was because morgues stood on river banks and included a large number of drowned people, many of whom were suicides; many suicides were insane, and many insane people, like criminals, have surprisingly large brains (Gould 1981:96).

Gould concludes his statements about Broca by noting that he spent a month reading Broca's major works and recalculating his statistics:

> I found a definite pattern in his methods. He traversed the gap between fact and conclusion by what may be the usual route—predominantly in reverse. Conclusions came first and Broca's conclusions were the shared assumptions of most successful white males during his time—themselves on top by the good fortune of nature, and women, blacks, and poor people below. His facts were reliable (unlike Morton's), but they were gathered selectively and then manipulated unconsciously in the service of prior conclusions. By this route, the conclusions achieved not only the blessing of science, but the prestige of numbers. Broca and his school used facts as illustrations, not as constraining documents. They began with conclusions, peered through their facts, and came back in a circle to the same conclusions. Their example repays a closer study, for unlike Morton (who manipulated data, however unconsciously), they reflected their prejudices by another, and probably more common, route: advocacy masquerading as objectivity (Gould 1981:85).

Stepan agrees with Gould that Broca and Morton were carrying out bad science, not pseudoscience: "Though many of the scientists who studied race in the past were indeed guilty of bias in the collection and interpretation of their data, of failing to consider contrary evidence, and of making hasty or facile generalisations, few of them knowingly broke the accepted canons of scientific procedure of their day. Most of them were not consciously racist" (1982:xvi). Stepan also believes that many scientists believed that the race problem was the key issue of their day, and that their science was bad because it was based on notions of typology, especially those dealing with skull measurements (1982:xvii).

She concludes that "Race science . . . is best understood not in terms of changing stages, but in terms of an underlying continuity . . . [predicated on] 'symbolic generalisations', allowing for 'shared expectations and judgments' about human diversity. . . . The scientists' deepest commitment seems to have been to the notion that the social and cultural differences observed between peoples should be understood as realities of nature" (1982:xx).

The natural historians used the race concept to arrive at appropriate taxonomic categories or boxes into which to put different groups, but those boxes were difficult and inexact because not all the members of a population necessarily had the traits defined by the boxes. The search began for the "ultimate" trait, a trait that would not vary from one individual or group to the next but would be constant, invariant. When this trait was found, the second or Darwinian phase of racial studies was launched; in this school, the notions of typology were combined with those of eugenics to produce a group that believed absolutely in the fixity of "racial" characteristics, together with the ranking involved (whites on the top, blacks on the bottom) and the additional notion that certain of those fixed characteristics rendered some members of the population "unfit" for civilized social life. The search for the perfect trait produced, at last, what was thought to be an immutable or unvarying characteristic: head form.

Applying their typological notions to head shape, the typologists arrived at the following conclusions:

1. Human heads come in two overall shapes, long and round. Europeans generally have long heads—or at least those who did the classifying were long-headed—and other peoples, they soon discovered, were round-headed.

2. Long-headedness and round-headedness were then found to account for many differences between groups. Naturally, if "we" were long-headed and superior, it followed that "they" were round-headed and inferior.

According to the typologists, head shape was the perfect indicator of capacity for civilization.

The typologies, originally built on classifications much like those of Linnaeus, were endlessly elaborated. Where Linnaeus had seen only a white race in Europe, Ripley in 1899 asserted that there were three races in Europe: Teutons, who were "entirely restricted to northwestern Europe" but were "perhaps the most characteristic"; Alpines, whose heads were "short and at the same time broad" [round, in other words]; and a third type similar to the Teutons in being long-headed but shorter in stature, found in the southern regions of Europe. The stature of this third type, Ripley thought, might be accounted for by "too protracted civilization" (Ripley 1899:121 et seq.).

Ripley's classifications led to more: only a year after Ripley published his findings, another researcher reported that 5,000 measurements could be carried out on the human skull. Head shape seemed the key to racial classifications, and the five thousand measurements were but a variation on the theme of the use of physical characteristics to justify social policy. One outcome of the discovery of this new immutable trait was restriction of immigration. It was argued that some people, by virtue of the shape of their heads, were incapable of civilization. But American anthropology, still in its formative stages, was to contradict the notion of immutability.

FRANZ BOAS AND AMERICAN ANTHROPOLOGICAL RESPONSES

George Stocking, Jr., leading historian of American anthropology, emphasizes the role of Franz Boas in contradicting the notion of immutability, using scientific data to discredit the belief that head forms were unchanging. Franz Boas (1858–1942) was born in Germany, the son of Jewish freethinkers, liberals who embraced, in Boas's words, "the ideals of the Revolution of 1848," including "equality of opportunity, education, political and intellectual liberty, the rejection of dogma and the search for scientific truth, identification with humanity and devotion to its progress" (quoted in Stocking 1968:149).

In completing his doctoral studies, Boas carried out what he called a "psychogeographical" study of the color of seawater and in the course of that study he lived with the Eskimos. Of this experience, he wrote:

> The little adventures of their life were my adventures, and I hope what my description may seem to be wanting in exciting scenes and imminent dangers will be made good by the fact that my experiences are those of a whole people, that my difficulties and dangers were such as the Eskimo have to brave and struggle with throughout their lives (first published 1887:383–402, quoted in Stocking 1974:45).

Stocking notes that anthropologists may have overemphasized Boas's switch from geography to anthropology, that Boas underwent no "conversion" experience in the course of his work with the Eskimo. Thus, says Stocking, "a large part of what he got out of his Arctic experience was simply confirmation of attitudes which in one form or another he had in fact brought with him" (ibid.). In his (1883 Letter Diary) journal, Boas sounded a bit like Wallace:

> I often ask myself what advantages our "good society" possesses over that of the "savages." The more I see of their customs, the more I realize that we have no right to look down on them. Where amongst our people would you find such true hospitality? . . . The Eskimo are sitting around me, their mouths filled with raw seal liver (the spot of blood on the back of the paper shows you how I joined in). As a thinking person, for me the most important result of this trip lies in the strengthening of my point of view that the idea of a "cultured" individual is merely relative. . . . (quoted in Stocking 1968:148; cf. Cole 1983).

Boas emigrated to the United States, where he became the "Father of American Anthropology," training the important figures of anthropology in the next generation—including Margaret Mead, Edward Sapir, Ruth Benedict, Robert Lowie, and Alfred Kroeber. He also made contributions to nearly all fields of anthropology and his major works included *The Mind of Primitive Man*; *Primitive Art*; *Race, Language and Culture*; *Dakota Grammar*; and *The Kwakiutl of Vancouver Island*. Boas was one of the most prolific of writers; at the end of his life, he chose sixty-two of his articles to be published in *Race, Language and Culture* (1940). By the end of 1911, Stocking says, there were four hundred entries in Boas's bibliography. Boas also corresponded with Booker T. Washington, Andrew Carnegie, and other influential leaders of the time (Stocking 1974:308) and spoke out on matters of public concern: W. E. B. DuBois invited Boas to address an assembly of black professional men in Atlanta in 1905.

His example was followed by the first generation of American anthropologists, people he trained and encouraged to participate in debate on social issues and policies. Stocking (1974) deals at some length with Boas's role in the propagation of anthropology and its application to social problems and suggests that Boas's view of race as a physical rather than a spiritual phenomenon (1974:15) was one of the viewpoints that was further elaborated in the anthropology of the 1950s and 1960s. Boas characterized racism as "based fundamentally on two misconceptions: the one, the confusion of heredity in a family and heredity in a population; the other, the unproved assumption that the differences in culture which we observe among peoples of different type are primarily due to biological causes" (1969:30). He also distinguished carefully between race, language, and culture: Stocking notes, "In each area what was involved was an attempt to show that the allegedly differentiating criteria did not march in lockstep, but were affected in complex ways by interacting historical processes" (1974:14). These viewpoints were to lead Boas to a lifelong involvement in controversies with all who believed that physical and cultural traits were inexorably linked—racists, eugenicists, anti-Semites, and others.

After Boas emigrated to the United States in 1884, he spent a brief time at Clark University, where he began the study of immigrant children. In addition to his liberal upbringing, Boas had studied with Rudolf Virchow, also a liberal and a scientist who was rather cool toward Darwinism generally and one of the few scientists of the time who specifically rejected the notion of racial inferiority. Of Virchow's work, Boas said that it had "little to do with racial questions," and instead dealt with "the influences of environment upon growth" (quoted in Stocking 1968:165). This was also to be the thrust of Boas's work, and in a letter to Professor J. W. Jenks, head of the U.S. Immigration Commission, Boas reiterated his concerns: "During the last ten years attention has been drawn to the change in composition of our immigrant population. Instead of the tall blond northwestern type of Europe, masses of people belonging to the east, central and south European types are pouring into our country; and the question has justly been raised, whether this change of physical type will influence the marvellous power of amalgamation that our nation has exhibited for so long a time" (Boas 1908). Boas proposed to the Commission that he study the head forms of immigrants, dealing with three basic problems: "the selection that was involved in the immigration process itself; the changes that took place in this country in children born abroad; and further changes that might take place in children born in this country" (ibid.:176).

The Commission's goal was to restrict immigration, but Boas's findings did not support their assumptions. Boas measured the heads of more than 18,000 European immigrants and their offspring and found, to nearly everyone's surprise, that round-headed immigrants to the United States tended to become more long-headed, as their stay in the United States lengthened. Immigrant round-headed parents produced children who tended to be long-headed; the first child of such parents, born in the "old country," might be the most round-headed of all the children; the second would be more long-headed, and so on through the youngest child, who would be the most long-headed.

This finding put the lie to the idea that long-headedness was inherently a measure of superiority, and eventually it also killed the idea that head shape was an immutable characteristic of the human species. All traits seemed to be influenced by environment and subject to considerable variation, 5,000 measurements or not. Nature appeared to delight in producing mongrels, not purebred types. This infuriated another group that opposed Franz Boas, the eugenicists, whose doctrines were popular in America from the beginning of the twentieth century. Boas's findings did not stop the eugenicists' attempt to translate racial dogmas into public policy.

Nor did Boas's findings lead the Immigration Commission to change its mandate: the Commission simply used other grounds as the basis for restricting immigration. Typological notions were discredited but not dead: Loring Brace notes that "typological thinking is alive and well and continuing to flourish in the last quarter of the twentieth century" (1991:49).

But the eugenicists could revive another idea to explain Boas's findings. Madison Grant, leading eugenicist, wrote:

> Dr. Boas, himself a Jew, in this matter represents a large body of Jewish immigrants, who resent the suggestion that they do not belong to the white race, and his whole effort has been to show that certain physical structures [head forms], which we scientists know are profoundly indicative of race, are purely superficial (quoted in Chase 1980:163).

EUGENICS IN AMERICA

Eugenics as an idea was first propounded in England by Francis Galton, Charles Darwin's cousin. Galton and the eugenicists believed that human races could be improved by promoting the selective breeding of individuals with "good" genes and discouraging breeding by those people who were lacking in good genes. The trick in such a program is deciding who has and who does not have good genes, but the doctrine of survival of the fittest made this an apparently easy decision. Like the idea of evolution, eugenics was adopted eagerly and initial attempts to implement it were made most readily in the United States. Allan Chase, author of *The Legacy of Malthus*, has written one of the most complete accounts of the eugenics movement in America, from its inception at the beginning of the twentieth century. He points out that Malthusian ideas, in combination with the social Darwinist idea that evolution proceeded by survival of the fittest, led to the belief that the "fittest" members of the population were those who had the most material goods, that the "unfit" were those who lived in poverty, and that evolution was acting to eliminate the poorest segment of the population. Since evolution acted slowly, societies could lend a hand to the progressive betterment of the species by eliminating charity or those programs designed to benefit the poorest people. These social Darwinist ideas were formulated in the absence of a precise understanding of the mechanisms of human heredity, and their applications were not impeded by the rediscovery, at the beginning of the twentieth century, of Mendel's findings about the mechanisms of inheritance. Nor was subsequent research on heredity immediately applicable to the concept of race; eventually, however, the new understanding of human heredity, in combination with knowledge of the Nazis' use of American eugenics laws, would lead most anthropologists to discard race as a scientific concept.

Chase believes there were four important figures in the American eugenics movement (1980:139): Charles Benedict Davenport, whom Chase describes (1980:114) as the movement's "pope"; Prescott Farnsworth Hall, who wrote extensively about the deleterious effects of immigration on the United States; Henry Herbert Goddard, who coined the pseudonym Kallikaks to describe an American family of degenerates who produced feebleminded offspring; and Madison Grant, author of *Race and Democracy* and specialist in anti-Semitism.

I will concentrate here on the activities of Charles Benedict Davenport (1866–1944), who began his career teaching zoology at Harvard. He went on to an associate professorship at the University of Chicago and soon persuaded the Carnegie Institution of Washington to fund the Carnegie Institution Station for Experimental Evolution at Cold Spring Harbor. He then convinced Mrs. E. H. Harriman to fund the Eugenics Record Office, and from these institutional bases, he proceeded to concentrate on supporting legislation to restrict immigration and to allow compulsory sterilization of people of "inferior blood," as determined by the eugenics office. He wrote to Galton that "In this country we have run 'charity' mad. Now a revulsion of feeling is coming about, and people are turning to your teaching" (Chase 1980:119). Charity, in Davenport's broad definition, included all private and governmental programs funded to improve public health, family health, occupational safety, and mental health. Davenport and Goddard trained a group of young women, some of whom were college graduates, as fieldworkers. The first training site, before the Cold Springs Harbor facility was completed, was the Vineland, New Jersey, Training School for Feeble-minded Girls and Boys: training involved some weeks of talking to the school inmates and a few weeks of lectures in eugenics. These "eugenics" fieldworkers were thus enabled

> at a glance, [to] spot and diagnose various hereditary mental conditions ranging from "dementia" and "shiftlessness" and "criminalism" to the most dangerous flaw of all, "feeblemindedness" (Chase 1980:121).

The fieldworkers' diagnostic techniques were described by one eyewitness as follows:

> Patients are selected, usually from an institution, and then their ancestry and relatives are looked up by a social worker [i.e., eugenics field

worker], usually a woman with very limited training in medicine, who goes into the community interviewing relatives, neighbors, friends, social agencies and studying records. This information is the chief basis for the conclusions reached, and to a medical man the sang-froid with which the social worker makes diagnoses on people she has never seen, or else met in a casual way, is nothing short of appalling. Really, it seems utterly unnecessary to have laboratories, blood tests, psychological tests, clinical examinations, and to take four years in a medical school plus hospital experience, etc., when a woman can as a result of a dozen or two of lectures make all kinds of medical, surgical and psychiatric diagnoses in an interview or by reading through a court record (Chase 1980:123).

In the early years of the twentieth century, eugenics laws to prevent the "socially inadequate" from procreating were considered in most state legislatures. Under Davenport's leadership, the Eugenics Record Office was active in the effort to have compulsory sterilization bills passed. In New Jersey, Governor Woodrow Wilson signed a sterilization bill in 1912, but the state supreme court found the law unconstitutional. In other states, such as Vermont, Nebraska, and Idaho, the governors vetoed the bills, and in Oregon one was repealed by popular referendum in 1913. There were some hold-outs, but by World War II, thirty out of forty-eight states had compulsory sterilization laws on the books. As of 1992, twenty-two American states still had these laws on their books (Finkelstein 1992; cf. Stefan 1989:417).

On the question of charity, the 1914 publication of the Committee to Study and to Report on the Best Practical Means of Cutting Off the Defective Germ-Plasm in the American Population first reviewed proposals for bettering the human condition and then announced:

It is held by some schools of social workers that better schools, better churches, better food, better clothing, better living and better social life will remedy almost any social inadequacy in individuals. The studies of this committee point strongly in the opposite direction. They prove conclusively that much social inadequacy is of a deep-seated biological [i.e., genetic] nature, and can be remedied only by cutting off the human strains that produce it. . . .

It is the bolstering up of the defective classes by a beneficent society that constitutes the real menace to our blood, because it lowers the basis of parenthood. . . . (quoted in Chase 1980:132).

Davenport himself observed that, although capital punishment was a crude way of dealing with those who sprang from criminal or defective lines, it was "infinitely superior to that of training the feeble-minded and criminalistic and then letting them loose upon society and permitting them to perpetuate in their offspring these animal traits" (ibid.:159–160). He also deplored the influx of the Irish, the Italians, and, worst of all, the Jews. In 1916 he gave an address called "Eugenics as a Religion," in which he quoted

Galton's hope that eugenics would someday become a religion and Davenport set out the Eugenics Creed:

> Eugenics has to do with racial development. It accepts the fact of differences in people—physical differences, mental differences, differences in emotional control. It is based on the principle that nothing can take the place of innate [genetic] qualities. While it recognizes the value of culture [i.e., nurture] it insists that culture of a trait is futile, where the germs [genes] of the trait are absent (Chase 1980:162).

To understand the influence Davenport and his colleagues had on American social policy, we can look at one example, as given by Chase, of Davenport's activities: his role in preventing scientific understanding of the cause and cure of pellagra. At the turn of the century, pellagra—now known to be a dietary deficiency disease resulting from a lack of niacin—was a serious scourge among the poor of the southern United States. Pellagra had been known in Europe for nearly two centuries and was first described by Gaspar Casal, a Spanish physician, in 1735. Even though Casal believed pellagra to be incurable, he cited an example of a peasant woman who, in the course of the melancholy deliriums characteristic of the disease, developed a great desire to eat butter; she sold all her property to buy butter and was cured.

Pellagra first appears as a skin disease, with rough red patches; in later stages it progresses to melancholia and insanity. It also weakens the individual's resistance to other common diseases, whether colds, influenza, pneumonia, or tuberculosis. In 1913, Drs. Siler and Garrison of the Pellagra Commission began investigating whether pellagra was infectious or communicable. They were soon joined by another doctor from the U.S. Public Health Service, Joseph Goldberger. Goldberger began by reading everything written about pellagra since the first publication of Casal's paper. Then he toured hospitals, asylums, mill towns, and slums in the south, as well as in New Jersey, Pennsylvania, Wisconsin, and Illinois. Chase says:

> Wherever pellagra was widespread, whether in institutions or in cities, Goldberger noticed two things: *Neither the professional nor menial employees of the asylums and prisons and county old-age homes had ever developed a single case of pellagra, and the disease never struck the nonpoor of Spartanburg and other mill towns where it was endemic among the mill hands and their families* [emphasis in original] (1980:207).

Goldberger was sure that pellagra was not communicable and he hypothesized that it was a deficiency disease. Goldberger injected himself and his medical assistant with the blood of a pellagra sufferer; neither developed the disease. Then he, his wife, and other doctors swallowed scrapings from the skin of pellagra victims, together with urine and feces of the victims. None of them developed the disease. Goldberger then persuaded a group of white convicts to live on a high-carbohydrate diet with no proteins or fresh vegetables for six months; they developed pellagra, which Goldberger promptly cured by feeding them the foods they had been without.

These findings were presented in 1915, but most of the doctors present at the medical meeting preferred the findings of another team of physicians who showed that pellagra was found in homes that lacked plumbing; this misleading correlation was accepted and Goldberger's proofs were dismissed as having "very little importance" (MacNeal, quoted in Chase 1980:211). Between 1914 and 1928, the reported pellagra deaths per year multiplied eightfold, from 847 to 6,523 (Chase 1980:212).

After accepting Goldberger's findings (presumably in the mistaken belief that the cure for pellagra had been established), Siler and Garrison left the Pellagra Commission; thereafter, control was assumed by Charles Davenport, whose previous experience was as director of the Eugenics Record Office. Davenport and a physician in his pay published articles asserting that pellagra was infectious, in accord with the findings of Siler and Garrison, even though Davenport was well aware that the two doctors had long since abandoned this hypothesis. He went on to claim that there was a hereditary factor in the way people responded to the disease: "This constitution of the organism is a racial, that is, hereditary factor" (1980:214).

In *Pellagra III*, the final report of the Pellagra Commission, Davenport mentioned and then dismissed in a footnote Goldberger's experiments on the ground that "the relative insusceptibility to pellagra of young adult men is generally recognized" (1980:216). Chase observes that

> As long as *Pellagra III* gave scientific authority to the lie that pellagra was a matter of bad genes and not bad diet, there were no impelling public health reasons for paying the poor southern whites . . .enough money to afford the fresh meats, dairy products, eggs, fresh fruits, and vegetables that both prevented and cured pellagra (1980:221-222).

Nor was there reason to intervene on behalf of those workers whose low wages did not allow them to buy pellagra-preventing foods. Pellagra continued to take its toll on whites and nonwhites until, Chase says, the beginnings of federal work and food relief programs in 1933:

> It is one of the crowning ironies of modern American history that, in the end, pellagra was to be conquered in the United States not by the wise and universal application of Goldberger's discoveries to American social policies, but, rather, by the fallout of the Great Depression of 1929–41.
>
> Suddenly the born (or undeserving) poor and the Depression-made (or deserving) poor were in the same boat—and it was the same federal relief programs that protected both classes of American poor from pellagra (1980:223).

One must ask if the outcome might have been different had Goldberger's name been Anderson or Jones; Davenport was on record as opposing the immigration of "hordes of Jews" (Chase 1980:161), and in later years defended

Hitler's plan to rid Germany of the inferior Jews by extermination (Chase 1980:634, n. 9). According to the authors of the Nazi eugenics laws, who thanked their American counterparts, their laws were modeled on the American laws.

In 1916, Boas—who had been an early supporter of eugenics—wrote an article on the subject for the *Scientific Monthly* and noted that although the idea of eliminating suffering by raising the standards of human physique and mentality was beautiful, its flaw was that only those features that were hereditary were thus eliminated and the interactions between heredity and environment were not yet understood. Thus "a false impression of heredity" was easily gained when environmental influences were far-reaching. Eugenics alone could not raise the standards of humanity because

> No amount of eugenic selection will overcome those social conditions by means of which we have raised a poverty- and disease-stricken proletariat, . . . so long as social conditions persist that remorselessly push human beings into helpless and hopeless misery. . . . Eugenics alone can not solve the problem. It requires much more an amelioration of the social conditions of the poor which would also raise many of the apparently defective to higher levels (1916:477).

Finally, Boas warned, "Eugenics is not a panacea that will cure human ills; it is rather a dangerous sword that may turn its edge against those who rely on its strength" (ibid.).

The American Anthropological Association, founded early in the twentieth century, was a professional association whose members mostly held doctorates in anthropology. Franz Boas served as its president from 1907 to 1908. Davenport and Grant deplored the professionalization of anthropology and determined to set up a rival anthropological society whose membership, according to Osborn's memo of 9 March 1918 would be limited "and also *confined to Native Americans*, who are anthropologically, socially, and politically sound, no Bolsheviki need apply" (Chase 1980:165). Not all its members were nonprofessionals: Earnest A. Hooton, Harvard anthropologist and Galton Society member, upheld the cephalic index. The Galton Society for the Study of the Origin and Evolution of Man was formally launched in 1918, with Davenport as its first chair. Chase says that it "helped retard the development of modern anthropology in America for many years" (1980:166). Another influence on American society was to be Madison Grant's book, *The Passing of the Great Race*, published in its second edition in the same year that the Galton Society was inaugurated. Grant's book attacked Boas's conclusions and reiterated that skull shapes were immutable.

The railings of the anthropological community against the cephalic index as indicator of capacity for civilization had little influence on popular ideas about race; eugenics, too, was a popular idea and it was to have its day. Oliver Wendell Holmes's famous statement, "Three generations of imbeciles are enough," is found in the 1927 majority decision in *Buck* v. *Bell*, in which the court upheld the right of the state of Virginia to sterilize Carrie Buck, daughter of Emma Buck, who had a mental age of eight years, and mother of seven-month-old Vivian, who was pronounced "not quite normal" (Baker 1991:599). Chase says of Holmes:

> When it came to the etiology of feeblemindedness, the brilliant and liber-tarian Justice Holmes was as one with the mediocre President Coolidge and the overtly racist editor of *The Saturday Evening Post* in accepting the pseudo-scientific hereditary theories of amateurs in genetics, psychology, and biology . . . and proponents of the long since disproven unit charac-ter theories of heredity such as Charles Benedict Davenport, as against the scientific counter-data of clinically and professionally qualified people like Dr. Fernald and the majority of American life and behavioral scientists.
> . . . Holmes and seven of the eight other Justices, including his fellow liberal, Louis Dembitz Brandeis, accepted the validity of the old scientific racism and its dogmas of eugenics and dysgenics. That is, they accepted as science the eugenic doctrines of human development, human mentality, and human worth as preached by the likes of Galton, Gobineau, Grant, Osborn, Davenport, Goddard, Brigham and Laughlin (Chase 1980:317).

Liva Baker, one of Holmes's biographers, observes that "The American public was at the time caught up in a eugenics craze. Since the earliest years of the twentieth century, lecturers, books by enthusiastic laymen as well as scientists, articles in law journals, newspapers, and magazines had popularized the idea that selective breeding could vastly improve the composition of the human race" (1991:600). Holmes was a "true believer" in these principles, having read Malthus's *Essays on Population* eagerly and become a "devout Malthusian" (1991:601). Holmes continued to be proud of the decision in this case, and, Baker says, Carrie Buck, sterilized in 1927, went on to marry twice, sing in the Methodist church choir, and work as a practical nurse until late in her life. Baker notes:

> Considerable doubt surrounds her imbecility today. In fact, she was said to display substantial intelligence as well as kindness, to be an avid reader and a lucid conversationist, even in her last days. Her daughter, Vivian, lived only eight years, but she, too, contradicted institutional and judicial estimates of her mental capacities. She went through the second grade in school and was considered by her teachers to be "very bright" (1991:603).

By 1968, Chase says, 65,000 Americans had been sterilized against their will in the states that passed such laws, and more than half of those had been labeled mentally retarded on the basis of IQ test scores. Today sterilization comes under the control of the federal courts, and its uses and abuses are sub-ject to very stringent regulations, but even so, these measures continue to be directed against minority women. One writer reports that "A 1973 study of New York voluntary and city hospitals revealed a disproportionate number of Spanish-speaking women being sterilized, almost three times greater than Black women and six times as great as White women. Those figures continue to rise" (Fleming 1980:19). A 1992 *Ms.* magazine editorial reported that one quarter of all Native American women had been sterilized without their consent (1992:21).

THE MODERN SYNTHETIC THEORY

The view that race could be defined somehow as a group's unique or distinctive possession of discrete genetic particles, or genes, came out of the rediscovery of Mendelian genetics and the attempt of anthropologists from the 1930s on to apply this new understanding of human heredity to human differences. These redefinitions usually featured such words or phrases as *gene pool* (or *frequency*), *statistical* or *variation*. William Boyd's 1950 textbook offered this definition of race: "a population which differs significantly from other human populations in regard to the frequency of one or more of the genes it possesses" (Boyd 1950:207). A later rendering by another author reads: "A race or subspecies is a genetically distinguishable subgrouping of a species distributed within a more or less localized territory that interbreeds with other subgroups of the species in areas of overlap or when brought into contact with them. The frequency of gene exchange between races is highest in the overlap zone and decreases away from it" (Loehlin et al. 1975:24). In his textbook, *Human Variation*, Stephen Molnar offers a similar definition of race: "a geographically and culturally determined collection of individuals who share in a common gene pool" (1992:347). (Richard Schaefer also uses this kind of definition in his discussion of racial and ethnic groups, as mentioned in the Introduction of this book.)

It is worth noting that the amount of genetic variability between human groups has been reliably estimated by population geneticist Richard Lewontin, who says that if the world's population were to be destroyed tomorrow, leaving only one small group in New Guinea, that small group would contain in its genetic makeup 98 per cent of the variability available to the human species as a whole (quoted in Gould 1981:323). In other words, almost none of the variability available to the human species would be lost if all but one small group of humans disappeared.

Some anthropologists (Bleibtreu and Meaney 1973) have called the phase of physical anthropology that began in the 1950s the "great correlation game." A physical trait was chosen, then plotted on world distribution maps along with its environmental correlates. Temperature, humidity, sunlight, together with information on physical traits—all were plotted and replotted, but the correlations were loose or, in some cases, nonexistent. Dark skin might be found in tropical rain forests or in deserts; people of short stature lived side by side with people of large stature in the same environment. Worse, no sooner was a correlation found in one place than its reverse was found elsewhere. The correlation game was an unrewarding and short phase in physical

anthropology. The next phase, human adaptability studies, has been more successful and continues its search for explanations of particular physical traits in
specific places.

HUMAN ADAPTABILITY STUDIES

The phase of physical anthropology from the 1970s on is sometimes called
"human adaptability studies"; it takes environmental variables as the beginning points and seeks the human physical characteristics that go along with
them. Most known genetic traits do not seem to influence, positively or neg-
atively, the adaptation of a given population to its environment.

In short, anthropologists still do not know what the adaptive significance
of most human physical traits may be, even after a hundred years of speculation and well over a hundred years of "scientific" investigation. But there
are some indicators and some good hypotheses about a few traits, such as skin
color variations and adaptations to malarial environments. Almost all traits,
however, are still under study and their adaptive significance is not fully
understood. For example, people living in extreme northern and southern latitudes tend to be short and squat, and those living in equatorial latitudes tall
and thin. This seems to have to do with heat conservation for the northern-
ers and heat dissipation for the southerners—but tall, thin Eskimos can always
put on an extra layer of clothing, and the Bantus and the Pygmies, respec-
tively the tallest and shortest groups in the world, live in the same tropical
environment. Culture interferes with all sorts of physical adaptations, and
human beings adapt through their culture to the physical environment, not
the other way around. Through studies of culture and environment, we know
a great deal more about how human populations adapt but almost nothing
about why the adaptations turn up when and where they do.

Skin color—with its possible correlates, ultraviolet radiation and vitamin
D absorption—is now under study. Human skin color is a polygenic trait,
that is, there is no single "gene" for skin color. Instead, the trait is influenced
by more than one gene (or loci, to use the current language), although the
exact number involved is not known. Skin color distribution generally ranges
from the darkest near the equator to the lightest at the northern and southern extremes of human habitation. This correlates with the strength of ultraviolet radiation: greatest at the equator, diminishing toward the poles. It is
well known that ultraviolet radiation causes the skin to tan, then burn, and
this can lead to skin cancer. Dark-skinned people have lower rates of skin
cancer, but the disease strikes people late in life, usually after their reproductive period, and susceptibility to ultraviolet rays will not explain *why* light
skin might evolve in northern regions, only that it *could* evolve there (Relethford 1990:155–156).

The reason light skin might evolve is found in the interaction of ultraviolet radiation and vitamin D production. In the times before vitamin D
supplements were available, and in the absence of foods such as fish oils that

are rich in vitamin D, most human populations got their vitamin D from the sun. Vitamin D synthesis depends on ultraviolet radiation, which is strongest near the equator. Too much or too little vitamin D can be harmful. Too much leads to vitamin poisoning or calcification of soft tissues; too little leads to rickets, which causes deformed bones, including deformed pelvic bones, thus interfering with successful childbirth.

The hypothesis about the evolution of human skin color is formulated in this way:

> In regions close to the equator where ultraviolet radiation is the greatest, darker skin serves to block the harmful effects of excessive vitamin D production. In areas farther away from the equator, where ultraviolet radiation is less, dark skin blocks too much and therefore leads to a reduction in vitamin D production. Natural selection thus produces a directional change toward lighter skin color, which would be adaptive in such environments (Relethford 1990:157).

Much work remains to be done on refining and ascertaining the validity of this hypothesis, but so far it is the best hypothesis put forth about why skin color might vary.

The physical trait for which there is clearest evidence of adaptive value is the sickle-cell or sickling trait, a blood characteristic that cannot be observed without blood tests. It is found in many parts of the world, including West Africa, Europe, India, and South Asia. Sickling is a form of hemoglobin protein, which transports oxygen to body tissues. Sickling is adaptive in a malarial environment, although the cost is high: sickling confers some immunity on certain members of the population. Those who do not have that immunity suffer from malaria, whereas those who have the sickling characteristic in double dose, that is, too strongly, die from sickle-cell anemia.

Each person has two alleles (imagine these as places on a gene or chromosome) for hemoglobin production; if that individual has two of the same, nonsickling alleles, then the person has no defense against malaria and may die from its debilitating effects. If the person has two of the sickling alleles, death from sickle-cell anemia will occur before the person reaches reproductive age. If the individual has one nonsickling and one sickling allele, however, that person will have considerable resistance to malaria. The sickling trait is adaptive in malarial environments, and was first identified, together with its cultural components, in West Africa (Livingstone 1958) and later found in other forms in other malarial environments. Frank B. Livingstone did this work without referring to the concept of race (1964); he used clines (geographic representations of biological variation) to chart the genetic variations in abnormal hemoglobins, and commented that

> Abnormal hemoglobins . . . are the first genetic system in man to which we can apply genetic theory in any detailed way. They also emphasize the important relationship between man's cultural and biological evolution.

The evolution of gene frequency differences has often been called "race formation." With reference to abnormal hemoglobin, such a label seems not only grossly inappropriate but false when the implications of the concept of race are taken into consideration . . . the distributions of the abnormal hemoglobin genes are not at all related to the traditional races of man. . . . If natural selection is considered to be one of the major factors contributing to the gene frequency differences which exist among the hundreds of thousands of human breeding isolates, then the gene frequencies will vary with the intensity of selection as do the abnormal hemoglobins and not with "race" (Livingstone 1964:699).

In our own decade, almost thirty years later, hypotheses like Livingstone's are still being formulated and are yielding considerable information about human variation—but not, as Livingstone said, supporting the idea of race. Instead these hypotheses help us understand human physical and cultural adaptations to many environments. While some anthropologists discussed and denounced older anthropological ideas about race, most physical anthropologists quietly turned their attention to other matters, investigating populations and adaptations without reference to racial typologies or notions of ranking.

RACE AND CULTURE

In the post–World War II anthropological canon, race referred to the physical or innate qualities of human beings, and culture referred to learned characteristics. This lesson was hammered home by a variety of scholars in a multitude of publications. The position was lent support by the historical events of the 1940s and the revelation that Hitler had murdered six million people who were classified by his regime as of "inferior" genetic heritage. The reaction to Hitler's genocidal activities caused a great many people, prominent anthropologists among them, to rethink principles of racial classification and to reformulate statements about what race consisted of. In Paris, 1950, the United Nations Statement on Race read:

> The term "race" designates a group or population characterised by some concentrations, relative as to frequency and distribution, of hereditary particles (genes) or physical characters, which appear, fluctuate, and often disappear in the course of time by reason of geographic and/or cultural isolation. The varying manifestations of these traits in different populations are perceived in different ways by each group. What is perceived is largely preconceived, so that each group arbitrarily tends to misinterpret the variability which occurs as a fundamental difference which separates that group from all others (Kuper 1975:343).
>   The biological fact of race and the myth of "race" should be distinguished. For all practical social purposes "race" is not so much a biological phenomenon as a social myth. The myth of "race" has created an enormous amount of human and social damage. . . . The biological differ-

ences between ethnic groups should be disregarded from the standpoint of social acceptance and social action (Kuper 1975:345).

This was the first of four such statements drafted by distinguished international academicians—sociologists, anthropologists, historians, economists, and political scientists among them. The second draft, from 1951, was written to correct some impressions left in the first, predominantly sociological statement, and to clarify the opinions of those "within whose special province fall the biological problems of race, namely the physical anthropologists and geneticists, . . . because the first statement was not supported by many authorities in these two fields" (Dunn in Kuper 1975:348). This draft stated that "Race is unanimously regarded by anthropologists as a classificatory device providing a zoological frame within which the various groups of mankind may be arranged and by means of which studies of evolutionary processes can be facilitated. In its anthropological sense, the word 'race' should be reserved for groups of mankind possessing well-developed and primarily heritable physical differences from other groups" and further, "Most anthropologists do not include mental characteristics in their classification of human races. Studies within a single race have shown that both innate capacity and environmental opportunity determine the results of tests of intelligence and temperament, though their relative importance is disputed" (Kuper 1975:35–351).

In 1964, the United Nations again issued a statement on race, this time "to formulate the biological part for a statement foreseen for 1966 and intended to bring up to date and to complete the declaration on the nature of race and racial differences signed in 1951" (Kuper 1975:355). This third statement was stronger than the first two:

> Many anthropologists, while stressing the importance of human variation, believe that the scientific interest of these classifications is limited, and even that they carry the risk of inviting abusive generalisations.
>
> Differences between individuals within a race or within a population are often greater than the average differences between races or populations. . . .
>
> Most racial classifications of mankind do not include mental traits or attributes as a taxonomic criterion.
>
> Heredity may have an influence in the variability shown by individuals within a given population in their responses to the psychological tests currently applied.
>
> However, no difference has ever been detected convincingly in the hereditary endowments of human groups in regard to what is measured by these tests. On the other hand, ample evidence attests to the influence of physical, cultural and social environment on differences in response to these tests (Kuper 1975:355–357).

Once again, in 1967, a statement was made, this one dealing primarily with racism:

A particularly striking obstacle to the recognition of equal dignity for all is racism. Racism continues to haunt the world. As a major social phenomenon it requires the attention of all students of the sciences of man.

Racism stultifies the development of those who suffer from it, perverts those who apply it, divides nations within themselves, aggravates international conflict and threatens world peace.

[A] conference of experts meeting in Paris in September 1967, agreed that racist doctrines lack any scientific basis whatsoever (Kuper 1975:360).

Boas's best-known student, Margaret Mead, observed in the 1960s that anthropologists' understanding of race had deteriorated, that the discussion of race differences conducted in the pages of *Current Anthropology* (1962–1964) "was scientifically inferior to the arguments that were marshaled decades earlier in a period when biological knowledge was far less sophisticated" (1968:3). She added that the edited volume she was introducing

> gives an indication of the present state of knowledge and research on problems of race, and it represents a response to the barrage of pseudoscientific statements which, since the Supreme Court desegregation decision of 1954, have attempted to prove the innate biological inferiority of the group of Americans who are socially classified as Negro. These statements, which have drawn on inadequate, discredited, and inappropriate evidence to make blanket statements about the Negro, often carry the names of those who have held responsible academic positions (1968:3).

Parenthetically, it should be noted that Mead herself was always reluctant to mix biological and cultural insights, as is pointed out in Renate Fernandez's (1990) treatise on iodine deficiency. Fernandez notes that Mead recognized a "pervasive underlying iodine deficiency" in a particular Balinese village; nonetheless, she argued four decades later that the proper focus of anthropological investigation should not be on individuals or communities succumbing to environmental or nutritional stress but rather on individuals and communities apparently impervious to it (Fernandez 1990:8).

One of the participants in the first two UNESCO conferences was Ashley Montagu, who followed up with a number of books and articles about race (Montagu 1964; 1975; 1977). Probably the best known of these works is *Man's Most Dangerous Myth: The Fallacy of Race* (1964), in which Montagu characterized race as "the witchcraft of our time. The means by which we exorcise demons. It is the contemporary myth. Man's most dangerous myth" (1964:23).

Montagu went on to review the ideas about race that most anthropologists held: "In nature there exists groups of human beings comprised of individuals each of whom possesses a certain aggregate of characters which individually and collectively serve to distinguish them from the individuals in all other groups" (1964:67). He quoted Morant's (1944) renunciation of this doctrine: "It seems to me that the time has come when anthropologists must fully recognize fundamental changes in their treatment of the problem of racial classification. The idea that a race is a group of people separated from all others on account of the distinctive ancestry of its members is implied whenever a racial label is used, but in fact *we have no knowledge of the existence of such populations to-day or in any past time*" (quoted in Montagu 1964:72, emphasis added). Montagu suggested, following Huxley and Haddon (1936), that ethnic group be substituted for race, "as a challenge to thought and as a stimulus to rethink the foundations of one's beliefs" (1964:380). The advantages of such a substitution would be that, although the term *ethnic group* implies a distinguishable group, it leaves open the question of how the distinction is made and recognizes the group's existence while eliminating "obfuscating emotional implications" (1964:379–380). (Montagu was writing decades before the phrase *ethnic cleansing* came to public attention.)

Thus the battle positions within anthropology were drawn before the end of World War II; after 1950, victory was largely—but never fully—conceded to those who believed there was no such thing as race. But old ideas continued to have their devotees; as the cliché says, "You can't kill a bad idea." After World War II, the eugenicists changed the name of their "science" and continued their efforts, while anthropologists continued their critique of concepts of race but with very different emphases in the definitions used. Further, social scientists still had to deal with important questions about race and biological determinism.

DISCUSSION QUESTIONS

1. Refer to the question in Chapter 2 about allegorical contents, values, ethics, and so on, and contrast monogenism and polygenism in this respect.

2. Construct your own typology of racial types by first selecting the two best-looking Hollywood actors you can think of; then compare your ideal types to the reality represented by your classmates. Explain why your classmates might not match the standards set in the typology.

FURTHER READING

George Stocking, Jr. has dealt at some length with Boas's role in American anthropology, as well as with race and its many ramifications. One of his earlier books is a series of essays (*Race, Culture, and Evolution*), and his collection of Franz Boas's essays (1974), as well as two of Stocking's many subsequent works, *Bones, Bodies, Behavior* and *Victorian Anthropology*, most directly address the questions discussed here.

Stocking, George W., Jr. 1968 *Race, Culture, and Evolution: Essays in the History of Anthropology*. New York: Free Press.

——— ed. 1974 *A Franz Boas Reader: The Shaping of American Anthropology 1883–1911*. Chicago: University of Chicago Press.

——— 1987 *Victorian Anthropology*. New York: Free Press.

——— 1988 *Bones, Bodies, Behavior: Essays on Biological Anthropology*. Madison: University of Wisconsin Press.

Two excellent books dealing with race questions from different perspectives are by Michael Banton (social science) and Studs Terkel (popular).

Banton, Michael 1988 *Racial Consciousness*. Essex, England: Longman.

Terkel, Studs 1992 *Race: How Blacks and Whites Think and Feel About the American Obsession*. New York: New Press.

5

●

Discarding Race,

Dealing with Racism

A s an analytic tool for measuring and classifying innate physical differences between human beings, race was a self-limiting concept, largely because its explanatory power was so limited. The limitations of the race concept have now been fully explored in anthropology, with the result that most anthropologists have discarded the concept and even the word, so that the term is seldom used by professionals nowadays, except in occasional textbook discussions of the history of anthropology. In effect, the outcome of several centuries of "scientific" or "pseudoscientific" exploration of the question of how humans differed was merely the certainty that humans *do* differ. The late twentieth century's understanding is that differences within populations may be greater than those between population groups.

DISCARDING RACE

Not all anthropologists agree that discarding race is a sensible move; in a survey done in 1984–1985, when asked to respond to the statement "There are biological races within the species *Homo sapiens*," 52 percent of cultural anthropologists disagreed, versus 42 percent of physical anthropologists (Littlefield et al. 1982:641–655).

Alice Brues, a leading physical anthropologist, stated in a recent paper the position for retaining the concept of race. She advocated clarifying the conceptual bases on which it was formulated; then, she says, "The real secret of teaching about race is . . . [to] give students so much information that they will never think of racial differences as simple enough that you can base any kind of practical action on it" (Brues 1992:4). In an earlier paper, she points out that "We had better be prepared to explain what is there and why, before we discuss what it does or does not mean," and warns that "race," not sex, is becoming this generation's taboo topic: "Now, when young people ask about 'race' and see a look of panic on your face they will simply fall back on folklore. . . . The alternative is to be prepared to discuss why different populations look different, which requires a knowledge of genetics; and how a race or subspecies can be described, which requires a knowledge of biological variation in general, statistics, central tendencies, measures of variance and the overlapping of distribution curves" (Brues 1991:5–6). Although I have a good deal of sympathy for this position, I have not found it the most practical approach to teaching students about the problems of race and racism. I believe there is more to be gained by firmly separating race from racism and then dealing with these as they have been used: race as a scientific concept was ultimately not useful, but race as an idea is based on folk taxonomies that are faulty, and racism—of several kinds—persists in American society and has many consequences.

One recent critic put the problem about race very well: "Reiterating that there's no such thing as 'race' offers only the frail reassurance that there *shouldn't* be a problem. It cannot deal with the problems that do exist, because it fails to see them for what they are" (Donald and Rattansi 1992:1). One has to go beyond simply denying that there is such a thing as race, or suggesting that differences do not exist, and, as Brues suggests, make the point that all attempts at classifying groups on the basis of physical characteristics, at ranking physical differences or at sorting them into typological frameworks—all carrying implicit notions of inferiority and superiority—have failed, despite almost two centuries of the best "scientific" efforts. In 1991, the American Anthropological Association had as its conference theme "Nationalism, ethnicity, race and racism," but—apart from Alice Brues's paper in a symposium on race—most of the discussions from that conference focused on nationalism and ethnicity, not race and racism. I think it is fine to discard the "scientific" concept of race and to point out that folk taxonomies and science have often been intertwined in the past but in this particular respect are so no longer. But I do not think it is sensible to disregard the very real problems that we all face because of racism.

Another question that must be raised is why, if anthropologists agree that race is not a viable scientific concept and that racism is an ongoing social problem, do we so often dismiss both race and racism as fit subjects for anthropological study? Within any academic discipline, there is room for intellectual disagreements about definitions and interpretations, as well as about what constitutes proper subject matter, but with race and racism, there is not so much disagreement as a muddled refusal to discuss the subject coherently.

Having taught introductory students for almost twenty years and been asked over and over by those students about the anthropological meaning of race, I take particular notice of the definitions and discussions of race and racism found in introductory anthropology textbooks. Earlier I discussed some popular sociology texts that continue to repeat outmoded definitions of race; here I will focus on anthropology texts, which have changed considerably from those of previous years (cf. Littlefield et al. 1982). In the 1970s, in-depth discussions of race and racism were commonplace, for example, Joseph B. Birdsell (*Human Evolution*, 1975) devoted one chapter to the question of regional variations in human populations and another to the relevance of race, discussing neoracist claims such as "race is real; some races are superior to others; IQ test scores prove that whites are superior to blacks, etc." These myths were dealt with in depth and the fallacious reasoning behind them was clearly set forth. In the same decade, Mark L. Weiss and Alan E. Mann (*Human Biology and Behavior*, 1978) provided a lengthy discussion of the differences between race as a biological and a sociological concept, and delineated the merits of a clinal approach (1978:492–503). In the 1980s, such discussions were adumbrated and now, in the 1990s, either the terms have disappeared completely or they have become one-sentence definitions that are afterwards ignored.

A hint about why this may be so lies in an apocryphal story that used to make the rounds among anthropologists, about an anthropologist in a major university who tested students for racist ideas before and after a course. To the instructor's horror, the students' racist ideas had increased during the course, despite a careful exposition of differences between human groups and an equally careful denial that these differences had any meaning in terms of cultural (learned) behavior.

There are several possible interpretations:

1. Students became aware of the scientific validity of "racial" differences.

2. Students felt more relaxed about admitting their prejudices.

3. The instructor did a poor job of getting the anthropological message across.

4. Admitting the existence of physical differences between groups leads or allows people to assign their own, other people's, or their society's meaning to those differences, despite cautions to the contrary.

5. Teaching of anthropological viewpoints is dangerous because it feeds the fires of racist thinking.

I first heard this story in the 1970s when the first interpretation was the favored one, but in this "politically correct" decade of the 1990s, the fourth interpretation may be favored, and the interpretation extended to suggest that no mention should ever be made of physical or other differences. As television likes to portray this message, we (humans) are all the same and the differences, whatever they might be, are insignificant (Lichter et al. 1991). An anthropological colleague, Nigel Barley, refers to this approach as "soft-core" anthropology, but the hard-core reality is that at the physical level, human differences *are* insignificant or, if they signify something, we scientists seem to be a long way from knowing what it is. What anthropologists have proved in the last century is that our "racial" classifications had nothing to do with those differences. What we must prove in the next century is that we can abandon the social attitudes intermingled with our mistaken applications of "scientific knowledge," and get on with the process of studying cultural differences and similarities.

Whatever the explanation for the existence of the story about the unfortunate anthropology instructor, I do not believe any one of the explanations suggested is correct or sufficient; I think the message we should take from this story is that in discussing racist thinking, anthropology has yet to focus on the most important problem, which is why humans so easily divide themselves into groups and then believe in or even fight for the existence of those groups. The answer lies somewhere in the understanding anthropologists already have of ethnocentrism, which as I said early on is much like belief in the stork: as people get on toward maturity, they discover that the reality is far more interesting than the myth. The reality of other cultures, other peoples, is also far more interesting than the myth. And racism is an extreme form of ethnocentrism, a kind of "hyperethnocentrism," as are religious bigotry, cultural prejudice, and class biases. The challenge of the 1990s is to discover ways in which people can be socialized as group members without identifying targets to persecute. These issues are among the most important of this and the next century. It is surprising that anthropologists have not followed through on their own ideas, especially because anthropologists have given to so many social science disciplines the techniques for investigating group identifications and how one group classifies another.

In my own recent cursory survey of introductory anthropology texts published in the last five years or so, including six in physical anthropology and five in cultural anthropology, I found the issue of racism dealt with in depth in four physical anthropology texts and in only one cultural anthropology text.

The physical anthropology text, *Evolutionary Anthropology*, discusses racism, or racist studies, and first defines racist studies as those in which individuals are characterized according to group properties and their worth evaluated on the basis of their membership in that group (Staski and Marks 1992:322–326). The authors go on to explain why racist studies are immoral: first, because they conflict with our own society's principles of equal rights for individuals, and second, because there is no evidence to indicate that human groups are different in any way that could be interpreted as "better" or "worse" (Staski and Marks 1992:325–326).

Harry D. Nelson and Robert Jurmain's text, *Introduction to Physical Anthropology* (1991, 5th edition), contains an excellent discussion of race as a failed concept and a brief discussion of racism, pointing out that "race," as it is popularly used, is more a sociocultural than a biological concept. That is, a group of people may be designated as a race regardless of their genetic traits. Thus, children of mixed black and white parents are considered black, though genetically they are as much "white" as "black" (1991:195). They add that

"Racism is a cultural phenomenon that has no genetic basis. That one race is mentally or morally superior or inferior to another has yet to be demonstrated" (1991:204). They end with a quote from Sherwood Washburn: "Racism is equally a relic supported by no phase of modern science. We may not know how to interpret the form of the Mongoloid face, or why Rh is of high incidence in Africa, but we do know the benefits of education and of economic progress. We know the price of discrimination is death, frustration, and hatred" (1991:204).

Another author of a leading physical anthropology text argues for the retention of the race concept: Bernard Campbell in *Humankind Emerging* (1992) finds the notion of race and racial differences important for several reasons:

> First, it provides us with many striking and fascinating characteristics of human groups. Second, the study can also indicate, to some degree, ancient, prehistoric relationships among different peoples. And third, the racial differences themselves are mostly examples of rather precise environmental adaptations, and so the racial differences illuminate our understanding of evolution, especially human evolution (Campbell 1992:498).

Campbell defines racism as the belief in the superiority of one or more races over others (1992:518) and focuses his brief discussion on the word *superior*, concluding that there is no biological justification for racist behavior, that people should be treated "solely according to their individual qualities" (Campbell 1992:518). He adds that "Where cultural and linguistic barriers are dissolved, racial differences fade into insignificance" (Campbell 1992:518) but gives no examples of societies in which this has happened. In fact, a previous paragraph seems to indicate that Campbell does not think this would be a desirable state of affairs: "Extensive racial intermarriage would eventually lower racial tensions, but our species would ultimately lose in racial variability—a desirable prerequisite for further evolution" (Campbell 1992:516).

Most anthropologists are not of this opinion; Loring Brace (1991, 4th edition), in *The Stages of Human Evolution*, another influential text, does not mention race in his extensive discussion of the human fossil record, prehistoric populations, and human adaptations to different environments. Brace's text is not intended to cover the whole of physical anthropology; the author has written elsewhere about issues of race and racism (see especially Brace 1964b).

Another textbook, *The Human Species*, by John Relethford (1990) treats race directly, defining it as "a group of populations sharing certain traits that make them distinct from other groups of populations. The concept of race is difficult to apply to patterns of human variation." Relethford goes on to outline the problems with the concept, dealing with them at length in a separate chapter, "Approaches to the Study of Human Variations," in which he gives arguments against the racist "explanations" provided for various social policies.

Although it does not treat racism per se extensively, Stephen Molnar's (1992) *Human Variation* is subtitled *Races, Types, and Ethnic Groups*, and the

book offers an excellent and careful discussion of human variation, predicated
on the definition of race or subspecies as "an artificial construct—a device of
convenience to enable the human mind to organize information from the
natural world" (1992:31). Molnar also gives numerous examples of scientific
racist studies and their faulty premises.

In my brief look at five cultural anthropology texts, Marvin Harris's
(1991) was the only one in which there was an in-depth discussion of racism
in Western industrial societies (1991:37–40; 46; 372–384). Harris also points
to recent studies that refute racists' claims and explanations for poverty based
on skin color and unequal abilities. He attributes the rise of the "New
Racism" in the 1980s in part to "the fact that Ronald Reagan's administra-
tions devalued civil rights, encouraged resentment against affirmative action,
and fostered racial polarization by cutting back on critical social programs,"
(1991:373) and goes on to explore a deeper level of sociocultural causation,
that of the "marked deterioration in the economic prospects of the white
majority" (1991:373).

One text that I adopted, Richley Crapo's *Cultural Anthropology*, had in
its first edition (1987) an extensive description of both evolution and the nonconcept of race; its second edition (1990), however, omitted those chapters
that dealt with evolution or race. Writers of most other texts content themselves with an old-fashioned or faulty definition of race, for example, "A **race**
refers to a group of people who share a greater statistical frequency of genes
and physical traits with one another than they do with people outside the
group" (Ferraro 1992:5). Then, as the author of this brand-new textbook,
Cultural Anthropology: An Applied Perspective, does, they move on and never
mention racism or its implications for modern societies. In his concluding
chapter on the future of anthropology, Ferraro discusses the cultural survival
of indigenous peoples, the study of complex societies (read the holistic study
of small ethnic neighborhoods), and the greater utilization of anthropological
knowledge, and ends with the claim that his text illustrates "how anthropological knowledge can be used to solve problems by architects, businessper-
sons, medical personnel . . . [and others]." I would not dispute this claim,
but I do think it is necessary to ask why racism is never even mentioned as
being among the problems we all face.

Another text, Emily Schultz and Robert Lavenda's *Cultural Anthropology*,
despite a glossary definition of race as "a social grouping defined by observable physical features which its members possess and justified with reference
to biology" (1987:375), uses the word *race* in several contexts with different
meanings and without bothering to define it in the text, beyond noting that
"Physical anthropologists invented a series of elaborate techniques to measure
different observable features of human populations—skin color, hair type,
body type, and so forth [in the hope of classifying] the world's people into
unambiguous racial categories" (1987:7). They add that "The traits tradition-
ally used to identify races all depend on external, observable traits, such as
skin color, which do not correlate well with other physical and biological

traits. The concept of 'race,' therefore does not reflect a fact of nature, but instead is a label invented by humans that permits us to sort people into groups" (1987:7). Later, however, they mention race and ethnicity as involving criteria of a biological and/or cultural nature (1987:247) and then thoroughly confound earlier discussions by using class, race, and ethnicity as near-synonyms, remarking that "The presence in a complex society of nonclass groupings based on race or ethnicity complicates, and may even contradict, a classification of people based on relative wealth, power, or prestige" (1987:251).

An even less illuminating discussion is provided by Daniel Bates and Fred Plog (1990:317), who in their index entry for race refer the reader to ethnicity and later explain that "References to race, as in 'racial equality' or 'racial discrimination,' are in fact usually references to ethnicity" (1990: 329–330). They proceed to discuss blacks and whites in several places (1990: 332–333; 343–344), without further qualification, although they also mention African-Americans once or twice.

Michael C. Howard's *Contemporary Cultural Anthropology* (1989) begins by describing ethnicity as a way of drawing we–they distinctions but goes on to suggest that categorization of humans according to "physical or racial characteristics" begins as early as prehistoric cave painting and adds—inaccurately, because race was largely a nineteenth-century invention—that "The concept of *race*, or categorization according to physical traits, is virtually universal, as is the belief that the features chosen for purposes of categorization parallel differences in behavior" (1989:273). Race and ethnicity are conflated in this discussion but the author does not say why he has done this, nor is enlightenment provided by the glossary definition of race as "a category based on physical traits" (1989:455).

These conflations and confusing discussions are disturbing. Apart from Harris, who discusses racism by reviewing the false claims that underlie racist belief, and Crapo (first edition), who discusses the fallacies of the nonconcept of race, other textbook authors are quite casual or negligent in their discussions. One mentions "statistical frequencies" without noting that these have nothing to do with what we call race; another claims wrongly that ideas of race are "virtually universal" and yet another suggests that race is "synonymous with ethnicity" while defining race as based on physical traits. If these were simply ill thought out discussions or minor errors on trivial issues, they would still need correcting but not major rethinking. These textbooks, however, are being published in the same decade in which the popular press is giving a great deal of serious attention to the issues of race and racism.

For example, the subtitle of Studs Terkel's new book, *Race*, (1992) is "How Blacks and Whites Think and Feel about the American Obsession." Other books on the same subject, with titles like *The Alchemy of Race and Rights* (Williams 1991), or *Two Nations: Black and White, Separate, Hostile, Unequal* (Hacker 1992) or *Chain Reaction: The Impact of Race, Rights, and Taxes on American Politics* (Edsall 1991) or *Faces at the Bottom of the Well: The Permanence of*

Racism (Bell 1992), and *Race Matters* (West 1993), are appearing hourly from the presses, debating whether racism is a constitutive element of American life, whether current racism is a more effective, more sophisticated means of domination, or whether the civil rights struggle was misdirected. Anthropology's seeming determination to write itself out of one of the most important discussions of the present era seems perverse and badly timed.

We have moved a long way from the 1960s and 1970s, when most textbook authors explained why race and racism were not sensible scientific concepts, to the 1980s and 1990s when even the discussion of race or racism can be considered superfluous by textbook authors. This explains why students have no defenses against the racist charges they hear, but it gives us no basis for helping students confront racism. The question remains: how to deal with racism and biological determinism? It is necessary to take up the various kinds of racism, including institutional and scientific racism, and ways in which they have been and might be confronted.

Margaret Collins succinctly stated the objections to the "scientific" definitions of race that fed notions of biological determinism:

> The "scientific" notion that humanity may be divided into discrete categories on the basis of genetic differences has effectively served as a groundwork for arguments that: link race to differences in performance on I.Q. tests; and further, that remedial education can serve no purpose in improving the learning capacity of certain groups of people when learning limitations are set by genes. . . .
>
> Perhaps the most dangerous social implication of scientifically proposed racial classification derives from the power of their supposed genetic basis. While individuals may "pass" through the boundaries of folk taxonomies by possessing or adopting a few superficial characteristics of other racial groups, the genetically-based system allows no such transfer. Since an individual cannot alter his or her complement of genes, each person is assigned to one category for all eternity (Collins et al. 1981:14).

Discarding race does not mean simply discarding the word—it also means rethinking the implications of racist thinking in what previously has been set down as fact. Michael D. Coe (1992) recently provided a splendid example from archaeological studies of the Maya hieroglyphs. According to Coe, most of the scholarly discussion of Maya glyphs was informed by the belief that "the brown-skinned Maya" could not have had a culture as complex as that of Europe, China, or the Near East (1992:138). This was the opinion of one man, Eric Thompson, who opposed the Russians who wanted to treat the glyphs as writing and translate them. Coe asks:

> Why did the Maya decipherment take so very long as compared to, say, Egyptian or the cuneiform scripts or Hieroglyphic Hittite? I am sorry to say that the major reason was that almost the entire Mayanist field was in willing thrall to one very dominant scholar, Eric Thompson, who by the

force of his personality, his access to the resources of the Carnegie Institution of Washington, his vast learning, and his acerbic—even cruel—wit, was able to stem the Russian tide until his demise in 1975 (1992:164).

Coe notes that Thompson's thinking was "quasi-racist" (I would call it racist) and adds:

> It seems that Thompson never believed that there was any system at all in what the Maya wrote down: it was a mere hodgepodge of various primitive attempts to write, inherited from the distant past and directed towards supernatural ends by the priests who supposedly ran the society. If he had been the slightest bit interested in comparative analysis, which he definitely was not, he would have found out that none of the "hieroglyphic" scripts of the Old World worked this way. Here he made a fatal mistake, for if anthropology teaches us anything, it is that at a given level of social and political evolution, different societies around the globe arrive at very similar solutions to similar problems—in this case, the need by early state societies to compile permanent, visual records of impermanent, spoken language (1992:260–261).

Such examples can be and are being multiplied regularly, as discussions of the meanings and implications of racism continue to move far beyond those of the 1960s.

DEALING WITH RACISM

Simply defined, racism "is the belief that humans are subdivided into distinct hereditary groups that are innately different in their social behavior and mental capacities and that can therefore be ranked as superior or inferior. The presumed superiority of some groups and inferiority of others is subsequently used to legitimate the unequal distribution of the society's resources, specifically, various forms of wealth, prestige, and power" (Marger 1985:16). As we have seen, race as an idea and the practice of racism preceded scientific discussions of what constituted a race and although those discussions lent credibility to the idea that races were real, the demise of the race concept has not led to the demise of racism, which seems likely to outlive its scientific justifications by a considerable margin.

Another definition is given by Allan Chase (following Webster) as "the program or practice of racial discrimination, segregation, persecution, and domination, based on RACIALISM," which in turn is defined as "the doctrine or feeling of racial differences or antagonisms, especially with reference to supposed racial superiority, inferiority, or purity" (Chase 1980:72). Defined in the most general way, racism is a special kind of prejudice, directed against those who are thought to possess biologically or socially inherited characteristics that set them apart.

Anthropologists may have been remarkably quiet on the subject of racism, but the few who have commented have had little to say that is flattering. For example, Stanley Barrett fulminates against the failure of anthropologists to deal with racism:

> Any list of major social problems in the contemporary world must include war and nuclear armament, welfare and poverty, sexism and racism, profiled against a common background of bureaucracy and elites. . . . The social anthropology of racism can be summed up in a few words: it has been a dismal failure. This failure has been due largely to the gross inadequacy of our theory. In the last part of the nineteenth century, anthropology was locked in a raging battle between biology and culture. Victory went to culture, which has been celebrated ever since as the hallmark of human existence. For reasons too obvious to dwell upon, we applaud the victory and rejoice in the flexibility of human social organization while reaffirming the basic mental identity of the world's variegated population, the realization that there are no superior societies, and the principles that the fundamental nature and capacity of the human brain is everywhere the same. But along the way we have failed to appreciate the degree to which racism continues to shape relationships among people. . . . Or, paradoxically, could it be that anthropology never really succeeded in disentangling racism from its biological connotation? To assume that racism evaporates with the victory of culture over heredity suggests such an interpretation (1984:222–223).

I believe, with Barrett, that we need a new theory of human behavior, one that concentrates on "problematic" aspects of human social behavior and emphasizes what we know to be characteristic activities of our species. One of the first characteristics that should concern us is the tendency of humans to divide into groups, to label one group (ours) the "in" group and the other (theirs) the "out" group. The challenge of the 1990s for all social sciences is to figure out how groups can maintain their social integrity without persecuting others. History shows us that it is not the definition of race or of any group as the "other" that does the damage; rather it is the implementation of racist ideas and the dehumanizing of the "other" that causes damage both to victims and to victimizers. It is instructive to look at how easily children learn discrimination.

There is a famous experiment in which eye color was the physical characteristic selected as the basis for discrimination. This experiment was conducted in 1968, by a schoolteacher, Jane Elliott, in Riceville, Iowa. The day after Martin Luther King, Jr. was assassinated, Ms. Elliott, after a long debate with herself about the best means by which to discuss and illustrate discrimination for her third-grade class, suggested to them an experiment:

> "Suppose we divided the class into blue-eyed and brown-eyed people," she said. "Suppose that for the rest of today the blue-eyed people become

the inferior group. Then, on Monday, we could reverse it so that the brown-eyed children were inferior. Wouldn't that give us a better understanding of what discrimination means?" (Peters 1971:20).

The class agreed and the rules were given:

"Today . . . the blue-eyed people will be on the bottom and the brown-eyed people on the top. What I mean is that brown-eyed people are better than blue-eyed people. They are more civilized than blue-eyed people. And they are smarter than blue-eyed people" (Peters 1971:21).

Elliott then went on with regular schoolwork but with some differences: brown-eyed children were helped when they made mistakes or praised when they did well, whereas blue-eyed children were disparaged by the teacher and ostracized by their classmates. Elliott then reported:

"By the lunch hour, there was no need to think before identifying a child as blue or brown-eyed. I could tell simply by looking at them. The brown-eyed children were happy, alert, having the time of their lives. And they were doing far better work than they had ever done before. The blue-eyed children were miserable. Their posture, their expressions, their entire attitudes were those of defeat. Their classwork work regressed sharply from that of the day before. Inside of an hour or so, they looked and acted as though they were, in fact, inferior. It was shocking.

But even more frightening was the way the brown-eyed children turned on their friends of the day before, the way they accepted almost immediately as true what had originally been described as an exercise. For there was no question, after an hour or so, that they actually believed they were superior" (Peters 1971:24–25).

On the following Monday, as promised, discriminated and discriminators reversed places. Now the brown-eyed children were the object of the teacher's scorn, and she said:

"I had not expected that the brown-eyed children, knowing full well after their experience on Friday that it was all an exercise . . . would react as intensely as the others had to the experience of discrimination. . . . But they did. Within minutes, they had become nervous, depressed, resentful. The only real difference that day was that the blue-eyed children, now on top, were noticeably less vicious in their treatment of the underlings than the latter had been to them" (Peters 1971:30–31).

Elliott repeated this experiment for several years thereafter, with much the same results in each class, and she reflected on the experience in this way:

"There must be a better way to teach children these lessons than the one I thought of. There must be a way to keep children from growing up into the kind of adult so many of us are, a way less drastic, less painful than this. And if we can get to the moon, we can certainly find it. There must be an expert somewhere who could tell me a better way to do this job. But so far, nobody has" (Peters 1971:47).

This experiment makes a simple but frightening point: by the age of eight, children are well able to assume the role of racial superior or inferior, no matter how whimsical the criterion for judgment, nor, as in the Iowa case, how limited their experience of other "racial" groups might be. Riceville was a small town with a population of 898, all of the same skin color. The results have been widely reported in the media, but the experiment has not been incorporated into many textbook discussions of racism—anthropological or otherwise—nor, so far as I know, has this or a similar experiment been incorporated into the teaching curriculum.

We must not only teach children about racism, we must also teach them about the consequences of discrimination or racist activities. It has been demonstrated over and over again, as it was here, that teacher expectations are an important component of all learning processes: when the teacher told the children what to do, how to behave toward their inferiors, and underlined these statements by berating the "inferior" group for failure, both the superior and inferior groups met her expectations. Sociologists call this a self-fulfilling prophecy; perhaps an even more frightening aspect of Ms. Elliott's experiment was how quickly the children began to act as if they were inferior, to behave in ways that guaranteed that others would observe them as inferior. This is called internalizing racist ideas or beliefs.

Gloria Yamato writes about internalized racism, which she defines as the point at which people come to believe misinformation about their particular ethnic group, thus believing their mistreatment is justified. She notes that

> Internalized racism is what really gets in my way as a Black woman. It influences the way I see or don't see myself, limits what I expect of myself or others like me. It results in my acceptance of mistreatment, leads me to believe that being treated with less than absolute respect, at least this once, is to be expected because I am Black, because I am not white. Because I am (*you fill in the color*), you think, "Life is going to be hard." The fact of life may be hard, but the color of your skin is not the cause of the hardship. The color of your skin may be used as an excuse to mistreat you, but there is no reason or logic involved in the mistreatment. If it seems that your color is the reason; if it seems that your ethnic heritage is the cause of the woe, it's because you've been deliberately beaten down by agents of a greedy system until you swallowed the garbage. That is the internalization of racism (1988:3–6).

Yamato goes on to advise those whites who want to be allies of people "of color" to acknowledge racism, to educate themselves about it, and to do so without expecting gratitude on the part of those who are the targets of racism; she suggests that those who are working through internalized racism should educate themselves about the forms of oppression and resistance and act on that education by pointing out racism wherever and whenever they meet it.

Yamato also advocates acknowledging racism and the ways it circumscribes and pervades people's lives, and dealing with it by reclaiming delight in one's own ethnic heritage, by finding or creating safe places in which to feel what has been repressed so as not to continue to act out the past in the present and future (1988:3–6). This is one answer to the question of how to deal with racism, which, as one Trenton State (minority) student pointed out, usually is not dealt with. Suzie Demosthenes (1991:9) analyzed the issue of multicultural diversity discussions in this way: she decided to boycott all racism-related lectures and discussions because nothing new was ever discussed in those forums. The outcome usually was that diversity was best promoted by making posters and eating ethnic food, and she adds: "Our campus community is so dysfunctional when it comes to racial issues we think we can eat and make it go away. Every time we have some kind of conflict, someone always proposes that we eat ethnic food. Stop hiding behind ethnic food!" (1991:9). She continues:

> We are not being honest with each other. In other words, we do not say what we mean and we do not mean what we say. We say whatever we think needs to be said to reassure everyone that everything is just peachy.
>
> If you sit a group of black students together without any white students in the room, I believe you will get the honest truth about their perception of racism and race relations.
>
> If you put a group of white students in a room without any black students, you will learn about what they feel.
>
> You put the two of them in the same room, you will get B.S. (1991:9).

In other words, after creating those safe places in which to talk honestly, minority and majority students must learn to come together and speak to each other honestly.

I would add to Yamato's injunction to educate oneself that one of the best things about the present decade's writings on race and racism and its emphasis on multicultural education is that there are now far more publications available by minority writers than ever before (see, for example, Cornel West's *Race Matters* [1993] or Bell Hooks's *Black Looks* [1992]). It is the responsibility of an educated person to be aware of the viewpoints of minorities—not necessarily to embrace or endorse them but at least to allow them the dignity of acknowledging their existence and their right to exist. Anthropology textbooks would do well to begin by acknowledging that racism exists.

SCIENTIFIC RACISM

There are other kinds of racism, including scientific and institutional racism. These are sometimes combined in the definitions and they have similar functions or aims. The heirs to many of the ideas first propounded by the eugenicists are called scientific racists or, less frequently, biological determinists.

Scientific and institutional racism are combined in Hunter and Whitten's definition of *scientific racism* as a

> term applied to theories that claim to demonstrate scientifically the inferiority of some "racial" or ethnic groups to others. Such theories generally argue that social inequality results from differences in intelligence between higher and lower status racial, ethnic, and class groups. Their major social implication is that significant inequality is inevitable or at the least that massive therapeutic measures are needed to raise the people at the bottom of the class pyramid to the level of their supposed betters.
>
> Opponents of scientific racist theory argue that it is not based on scientific evidence but is rather an ideological defense of the social elite. By blaming inequality on those oppressed by it, the ideology is said to rationalize society's biased allocation of power and wealth (1976:328).

They also point to two main schools of scientific racist thought:

> Scientific racism in the United States currently appears in two distinct forms—geneticist and environmentalist. On the one hand, a school of hereditarian psychologists led by Arthur Jensen claims on the basis of IQ test results that blacks and certain other oppressed groups are genetically less intelligent than whites. On the other hand, a number of academics, including such prominent men as Daniel Moynihan and Edward Banfield, have argued that lower-class groups, especially blacks, suffer from psychological and intellectual deficits due not to genetic factors but to disrupted family life and other damaging environmental influences (1976:328).

Scientific racism, as Allan Chase defines it, also combines the institutional dimension: "the creation and employment of a body of legitimately scientific, or patently pseudoscientific, data as rationales for the preservation of poverty, inequality of opportunity for upward mobility, and related regressive social arrangements" (Chase 1980:2). Chase believes that scientific racism came into being in 1798 in order to do one thing:

> That function was to preserve the type of social arrangements that had prevailed before the writing of the Constitution of the new United States of America made the establishment of equal justice and the promotion of "the general welfare" two of the basic functions of the state itself (1980:2).

He continues:

Scientific racism stands as a classical example of the life-wrecking powers of a single bad idea. That idea . . . is the pseudo-genetic simplism that everything about a person's condition in life—from his socioeconomic status and his educational achievement to his life span and the quality of his health—is immutably preformed in the genes he inherits from his parents at the moment of his conception (1980:5).

Another definition is Ladner's: institutional racism is "the set of policies, priorities, and functions of an ongoing system of normative patterns which serves to subjugate, oppress, and force dependence of individuals or groups by: (1) establishing and sanctioning unequal goals; and (2) sanctioning inequality in status as well as in access to goods and services" (quoted in Curtis 1975:18).

Peter Rose offers a slightly different definition of institutional racism:

The principal source of prejudice against nonwhite peoples. . . . The core argument is that a faulty belief in their own superiority is deeply ingrained in the minds of white people and in their social mores. They have internalized the same views as those promulgated by the protoanthropologists and perpetuated by those who, for several centuries, claimed to be lifting and carrying "the white man's burden." The late Whitney M. Young put it succinctly when he wrote that "racism . . . is the assumption of superiority and the arrogance that goes with it" (Rose 1974:120–121).

A more recent definition of individual versus institutional racism is given by Margaret Andersen and Patricia Collins:

Individual racism is one person's belief in the superiority of one race over another. Individual racism is related to prejudice. . . . Institutional racism is more systematic than this . . . a system of beliefs and behaviors by which a group defined as a race is oppressed, controlled, and exploited because of presumed cultural or biological characteristics (1992:49).

An alternate term for scientific racist thinking is *biological determinism*, which Lewontin (1978:319) defines as the assertion that although some minor improvements may still be possible in spreading status, wealth, and power, there is a limit to how closely equality can be approached—a limit set by the nature of the human species.

Biological determinism as an ideology has two seemingly contradictory facets, both of which are complementary and necessary to the complete argument. First, biological determinists claim that differences in status, wealth, and power among individuals and among groups are the result of genetic differences in abilities, personalities and behaviors. . . . [They also argue] that superimposed on the biological differences between individuals in ability is a tendency toward biological uniformity in behavior. Together, these biological qualities guarantee . . . that societies will always be hierarchical (1978:319).

Stephen Jay Gould devotes most of his book, *The Mismeasure of Man*, to examples of biological determinism, citing the data-collecting techniques of nineteenth- and twentieth-century researchers such as Samuel George Morton and Paul Broca, already mentioned, and Cyril Burt, whose data he also reexamined. The case of Cyril Burt most clearly illustrates the principles and fallacies of biological determinism. Sir Cyril Burt's findings had enormous influence during his lifetime (1883–1971), but his conclusions and evidence have been largely discredited since his death. Burt was committed to the hereditarian (biological determinist/scientific racist) idea that certain capacities and talents were innate. His proof came from his studies of identical twins separated at birth and reared in different homes. In later life, tests showed that all the twins had similar IQ scores, regardless of the environments in which they were reared; Burt claimed to have this data for fifty-three pairs of twins. His ideas that nature was the strongest component in IQ scores, and that intelligence was innate, had tremendous influence on the 1944 Education Act in Britain in which three kinds of schools were established—for those who would continue on to university education, for those who would be given vocational training, and for those who would be given other kinds of nontechnical education. Determination of which students went where was made with one examination, administered at age eleven.

After his death, admirers began to examine Burt's data and found that he had fabricated it; his "data" on identical twins, kinship correlations in IQ, and declining levels of intelligence in Britain were nonexistent. "The crucial charge against Burt concerns the figures he cites in support of his theories and the ways in which he arrives at them. During his lifetime, he made a classic study of separated twins from which he was able to make apparently controlled measurements of intelligence and genetic factors" (Gillie 1977:469). But no supporting data for this study have been found. Leon J. Kamin, Princeton professor, became suspicious of Burt's evidence about identical twins reared in separate households and he went to Britain to research what he thought might be a body of primary documents supporting Burt's assertions. He found nothing (Kamin 1974; Piel 1978).

According to Gillie (1977), there are other charges against Burt: first, that two of Burt's collaborators who were named as authors of research papers may never have existed, and that Burt himself wrote the papers and published them in journals that he edited. Burt indicated that the collaborators were his students, but the two he mentioned, Margaret Howard and J. Conway, were never registered at any university at which he taught. Further,

> Burt's housekeeper, Grete Archer, . . . distinctly recalls that Burt himself wrote the papers which appeared under the names of Howard and Conway, because she discussed it with him when the papers appeared. She says: "Prof said that since Miss Howard and Miss Conway did the research, it was only fair that their names should be on the papers." [Archer] never met Howard or Conway. She says Burt told her they had both emigrated and never sent their new addresses (Gillie 1977:470).

Second, his statistics are impossibly precise: "Burt miraculously produced identical answers accurate to three decimal places from different sets of data . . . a statistical impossibility . . . he could have done it only by working backwards to make the observations fit his answers" (Gillie 1977:469).

Gould says of Burt:

I think that the splendid "official" biography of Burt recently published by L. S. Hearnshaw has resolved the issue so far as the data permit . . . Hearnshaw has convinced me that the very enormity and bizarreness of Burt's fakery force us to view it . . . as the actions of a sick and tortured man. (All this, of course, does not touch the deeper issue of why such patently manufactured data went unchallenged for so long, and what this will to believe implies.) (Gould 1981:236)

Modern social scientists might do well to spend time thinking about the deeper issue Gould points to: why data that was "patently manufactured" went unchallenged. Institutional and scientific racism or biological determinism have had enormous and far-reaching consequences for our society, and we must consider whether we want to allow those effects (and their underlying assumptions) to continue and be perpetuated into the next century. Historians may well characterize the twentieth century as one preoccupied with race and unable to come to terms with racism; I want students to think deeply about the realities and effects of racism in America, because it is today's students who will have tomorrow's votes and who will have to live with and—I hope—correct this century's mishandling of issues and ideas.

Anthropologists have dealt with the IQ controversy time and again and in the most excruciating detail—Stephen Jay Gould deals with this question at some length in *The Mismeasure of Man* (1981). For two anthropological viewpoints, see Ashley Montagu, ed. 1975, *Race and IQ* and John C. Loehlin et al. 1975, *Race Differences in Intelligence*. But the point about IQ tests is simply made: "intelligence," however it is measured, is a cultural characteristic, related to an individual's grasp of the testmaker's categories and ideas. There is no such thing as a "culture-free" test, any more than there is a culture-free testwriter: the more a person knows of the testmaker's (presumably dominant) culture and expectations, the better the person's scores on an IQ test. Wherever and whenever efforts have been made to teach members of minority groups what they need to know about the dominant culture, those minorities score as well on IQ tests as any other group. The nature/nurture controversy perpetuated by the biological determinists is a false controversy, predicated on erroneous assumptions about the heritability of cultural traits.

DECONSTRUCTING RACE

Some anthropologists and sociologists are "deconstructing" the concept of race and studying the ways in which the word or idea is used. This involves, first, studying how the meanings of race have changed and, second, considering the many uses to which the idea is currently put. Sociocultural anthropologists study race as a sociocultural construct, as an idea that is not a constant, not based on physical realities, but one that varies from society to society, according to historic or other circumstances. Daniel Segal (1991:7–9), for example, deconstructs the notion of the "European" as an amalgam of retellings of colonial allegories intertwined with national boundaries. Segal illustrates by tracing the emergence of the category "European," as it intertwined with the notion of racial purity. Europeans, in American colonial times, meant white and this notion came to be associated with people whose ancestors were exclusively ("purely") white, especially when legal definitions about "drops of Negro blood" were added to the mix. Segal contrasts the American view with the West Indian view: in America, a "coloured" person is anyone of a skin color other than white, whereas in the West Indies, skin color vocabularies are much more elaborate. He notes that people are referred to according to their color mixtures: thus a "Trinidad white" was not someone of pure European ancestry but rather a person who was a marked and modified "white." Everyone is considered to be "coloured" but "particular colour terms ('white', 'red', 'brown', 'light black', 'black', 'black black') were used to identify the relative proportion of 'African' and 'European' ancestors in particular 'coloured' persons" (Segal 1991:8).

In postmodern terms, color is a metonym, that is, the use of the name of one object or part to stand for the whole, as when we say "counting heads" when we mean counting people. As a racial term, *color* stands for whatever other characteristics we assume are "racial" in origin. Many Americans include characteristics such as nose form, lip shape, or hair type in the set of characteristics subsumed as "color" and ignore other characteristics that some societies give importance to, such as stature. The fourth definition of color given in *The Random House Dictionary of the English Language* (1983:291) is "racial complexion other than white." Another dictionary gives as the twelfth definition of color, "skin pigmentation esp. other than white characteristic of race" (*Webster's Ninth New Collegiate Dictionary* 1986:261). Under *colored*, the third definition is "a: of a race other than the white; esp: NEGRO b: of mixed race" (ibid.). These are the uses that underlie American "biracial" ideas.

Another set of principles is brought into play in constructing the "Other." This construction, which occurs in all societies and is an outgrowth of ethnocentric ideas inculcated in the socialization process, has a number of common features, no matter what ethnic group does the defining of "us" and "them." One common assumption is that the Others are "dirty"—we are clean and they are dirty. Another is that they are childish or foolish or backward, whereas we are clever adults. Yet another is that they are inclined to incest or cannibalism, which we, as properly socialized humans, abhor.

Identification of the Other in the Euroamerican case is complicated by a long-standing association of darkness with evil; this is a Eurocentric idea, not a universal one. One has only to think of the various color metaphors that we use daily to describe odd or unfortunate individuals, activities, or events: black sheep, blackball, Black Monday, blackmail, black markets, and so on. This unhappy association makes it easier for us to see people as white or black when we are all probably better, more accurately, described as pink or brown. Pink and brown have no particular salience for us, whereas black and white as a set has considerable meaning in the Western world.

Other people have different ideas, usually based on ethnocentrism. The people I study in West Africa believe that we (Kom) people are better than them (any other Cameroonian or West African group) because the Kom were "chosen" by supernatural forces to be where and who they are. They also believe that Kom men are "better" than any others due to a combination of intelligence and sexual prowess and that Kom women are better than any others due to their beauty and their devotion to hard work. In addition, they consider their (matrilineal) kinship system to be the best possible system and have a saying that can be roughly translated as "Everybody else was behind the barn door when kinship systems were being handed out, so we got the best system"; that is, most other people ended up having to inherit property from their fathers instead of inheriting it "properly," through their mothers. These are not unusual beliefs; in fact, such notions of superiority are commonplace and found in one form or another in all societies. They are ways of constructing identities—both one's own and that of the other. As Kom people grow up and travel, they reformulate these ideas and revise them according to new experiences.

THE ROLE OF ANTHROPOLOGISTS

Anthropologists must go beyond defining racism and ethnocentrism: we need to describe these, in their various manifestations, with greater care. In all anthropological monographs, there ought to be discussion of the ethnocentric attitudes people subscribe to and the ways in which these attitudes are talked about, defended, and enforced, and what, if anything, is done about them. Margaret Mead was severely criticized by the people of Samoa for presenting as "facts" the culturalist/racist attitudes the people she studied held about their neighbors. So she should have been; but this criticism could have been avoided if Mead had incorporated into her monograph a description of the ways in which the people she studied defined themselves and how they defined those "Others."

Margaret Hodgen provides criticism of a different aspect of current anthropological theory. It is Hodgen's idea that current anthropological notions of "social evolutionism," or progressivism, developmentalism, and so on, depend on "earlier hierarchical notions of arrangement; and that these notions, together with an inflexible Europocentrism, have consistently belittled the mentality of the aborigine by installing him at the bottom of some scale of being" (Hodgen 1964:483). She quotes E. B. Tylor, one of the nineteenth-century founders of anthropology, as having said almost a hundred years ago that the educated world of Europe and America had practically settled the matter of superiority/inferiority "by placing its own nations at one end of the social series, and the savage tribes at the other, arranging the rest of mankind between these limits according as they correspond more closely to savage or cultural life" (Hodgen 1964:483).

Hodgen cites as example the discussion between the social evolutionists of the nineteenth century about which human group was the lowest, hence oldest. Darwin's choice, of course, would have been the Fuegians, as we have seen; others preferred the (!Kung) Bushmen of the Kalahari Desert, the Australians and Tasmanians, the Andaman Islanders, the American Root-Diggers or, in the French case, the Laplanders (Hodgen 1964:510). Lévi-Strauss (1976:342) offers a different example: he points out that we judge societies according to their technological prowess, that is, according to the areas in which we excel, whereas if we judged them according to different criteria— say, successful adaptation to difficult environments—our societies would not fare well when compared with the Eskimos or the inhabitants of tropical rain forests.

With Hodgen, I believe that Eurocentric notions of social evolutionism have militated against anthropological understanding of the impact of racism. Further, I question whether the discarding of race and racial typologies has been a paradigm shift in anthropology, a shift to different questions, or whether there has just been modification of certain basic assumptions that still carry built-in typological assumptions. We need to study these questions, in addition to those of in-group/out-group definitions, and to think deeply about the effects of racism on our society.

Anthropologists also need to describe what is accomplished and what is impeded by racist tactics: we know that they explain social and other inequalities as rational outcomes (by blaming the victims); that they enhance definitions of in-groups and inculcate ethnocentrism; that they help to legislate and sanction discrimination; that they reduce confusion about the role and status of strangers and how to treat people whose life-styles are widely divergent from our norm. What is impeded by racist tactics is the extension of equality to all, however *all* may be defined; the loss of the human potential for genius that anthropologists have witnessed in all societies; and the loss of understanding of how peaceful interactions can occur between groups whose ideas and backgrounds are very different from our own. Anthropologists also need to spend more time documenting the effects of racism: in education, in politics, in economy—how much does it cost to keep part of the population "in its place"?

One way to begin is to ask how different the world would be if race had never been invented—and how different it would be if racism were not the basis of so many social policies. Margaret Collins noted that it is the myth of race that keeps people apart: "The reification of an ideological construct called race restricts gene flow and random mating between populations,

inhibiting the admixture that might otherwise render us racially indistin-
guishable from one another" (Collins et al. 1981:17, n. 2). Would we be better protected against harmful ultraviolet radiation if our ancestors had
acknowledged the products of their "illegitimate" unions, if people of African
descent had intermingled freely with those of European descent, and our population today was neither "white" nor "black"?

On the question of racist social policies, Jonathan Kozol, reviewing public education in America, makes an interesting comparison:

> One way of establishing the value we attribute to a given group of chil-
> dren is to look at the medical provision that we make for them. The usual
> indices of school investment and performance—class size, teacher salaries
> and test results—are at best imperfect tools of measurement; but infant
> survival rates are absolute.
>
> In central Harlem, notes the *New York Times*, the infant death rate is
> the same as in Malaysia. Among black children in East Harlem, it is even
> higher: 42 per thousand, which would be considered high in many Third
> World nations. "A child's chance of surviving to age five," notes New
> Jersey Senator Bill Bradley, "are [sic] better in Bangladesh than in East
> Harlem" (1991:115–116).

> Kozol concludes: "Surely there is enough for everyone within this coun-
> try. . . . All our children ought to be allowed a stake in the enormous rich-
> ness of America. Whether they were born to poor white Appalachians or to
> wealthy Texans, to poor black people in the Bronx or to rich people in Man-
> hasset or Winnetka, they are all quite wonderful and innocent when they are
> small. We soil them needlessly" (1991:233).

If there were no such thing as racism or biological determinism, would
we have a better public school system, better health care delivery systems?

THE RESPONSIBILITY OF SOCIAL SCIENTISTS

I said in the introduction to this book that one of my reasons for writing the
book is the belief that anthropologists have abandoned their responsibility to
help people understand not just the meanings attached to the notion of race
but the meanings and social costs of racism as well. These social costs should
be thoroughly explored in every introductory social science course.

Fried observed long ago that "Science has no social responsibilities, but
scientists must accept social responsibility or face the consequences" (1968:
130). Anyone today who takes a course in comparative or "multicultural"
studies must learn the meanings of racial, cultural, religious, or ethnic prejudice and bigotry. They should be very clear about what those terms mean and
do not mean and what the outcomes of discrimination have been in the past.
Barrett is right when he says, "We have failed to appreciate the degree to
which racism continues to shape relationships among people" (1984:223). I
believe it is part of anthropology's responsibility to investigate the implications

of racism, and to help those we educate to understand the meanings and outcomes of terms we have done so much to define, terms such as *ethnocentrism*,
racism, and *bigotry*.

Another thing this book should have made clear is that anthropologists
in particular and social scientists in general have something more to contribute
to the understanding of these questions. Anthropology has already contributed
the technique of studying the ways in which attitudes are inculcated, but too
little use has been made of this technique and the results it has produced are
too little known. The South African novelist Doris Lessing remarks, "I believe
that people coming after us will marvel that on the one hand we accumu-
lated more and more information about our behaviour, while on the other,
we made no attempt at all to use it to improve our lives" (1987:20).

The major lesson I hope students will take away from this book is that
when dealing with race or racism "the appeal to scientific authority," as Banton calls it (1975:150), will not work, that "no major social implications auto-
matically flow from biological findings, and that therefore the meaning people come to attach racial differences depends upon political decisions"
(1975:153). But just for good measure, it is worthwhile to revisit the century's most infamous racist, the man responsible for exterminating six million
people in the name of racial purity.

As we have seen, Hitler knew that scientific talk about race was non-
sense, and he has already been quoted as saying that he was unconcerned with
the "meaning" of race in physical or sociological terms. Hermann Rauschning, who recorded his conversations with Hitler in the years before he seized
power and in the first two years (1933–1934) of the National Socialist regime,
was explicit about this in describing Hitler's interest in Sweden: "One thing,
however, is certain: Hitler is not interested in the pure Aryan blood of the
Scandinavians, nor in the northern myths of Viking heroism. He is interested
in the iron-ore mines" (Rauschning 1940:141).

Rauschning continues by discussing Hitler's notions about the Jews,
pointing out that although Hitler did indeed believe that Jews were "evil
incarnate" (1940:235), he also knew that anti-Semitism was a useful revolu-
tionary expedient, of which he made use:

> "My Jews are a valuable hostage given to me by the democracies. Anti-
> Semitic propaganda in all countries is an almost indispensable medium for
> the extension of our political campaign. You will see how little time we
> shall need in order to upset the ideas and the criteria of the whole world,
> simply and purely by attacking Judaism. . ."
> I asked whether that amounted to saying that the Jew must be
> destroyed.
> "No," he replied. "We should have then to invent him. It is essential
> to have a tangible enemy, not merely an abstract one." (1940:236–237).

There would be little point in recalling these manipulative statements if
Hitler's ideas had no currency in some circles. Race and racist ideas have for

many years served as a platform, as a device, for those who wanted power, and we have seen over and over in history that the increase in human rights in one place is often accompanied by their diminution in another. We must watch those shifts carefully and evaluate both the shifts and our own actions for what they are and may become.

DISCUSSION QUESTIONS

1. Identify whether the following quotations are relativist, racist, scientific racist, bigoted, or xenophobic. Note that the distinctions are not always clear. Discuss your interpretations with other students.

   The peoples of cold countries generally, and particularly those of Europe, are full of spirit, but deficient in skill and intelligence; and this is why they continue to remain comparatively free, but attain no political development and show no capacity for governing others. The peoples of Asia are endowed with skill and intelligence, but are deficient in spirit; and this is why they continue to be peoples of subjects and slaves. The Greek stock, intermediate in geographical position, unites the qualities of both sets of peoples. It possesses both spirit and intelligence: the one quality makes it continue free; the other enables it to attain the highest political development, and to show a capacity for governing every other people—if only it could once achieve political unity (Aristotle, paraphrased in Barker 1948:347).

   Investigation has proved that the smoothness of the brain and the pigment of the skin go hand in hand. There are exceptions to this rule but they are in the minority. Mental activity has the effect of convoluting the brain and the greatest number of convolutions are found in the brains of individuals of the races with the lightest skins; growing less through the gamut of pigments to the black, at which stage the brain has a smooth surface (Tobias 1972:25).

   The gift of narrative, with a sense for describing events and landscape and a tendency to roguish humour, is common in the Nordic race. . . . Fairness and trustworthiness are peculiar Nordic virtues. . . . Passion . . . has little meaning for him. In contrast, the Mediterranean man is very strongly swayed by the sexual life, at least he is not as continent as the Nordic. . . . Alpines are "petty criminals, small time swindlers, sneak-thieves and sexual perverts"; whereas Nordics are capable of the "nobler crimes" (H.F.K. Gunther, quoted in Tobias 1972:27).

   Then, with the sun straight up over their heads, they trotted off, leaving the sheriff behind among the damndest bunch of coons they'd ever seen. All testimony to the results of a little so-called freedom imposed on people who needed every care and guidance in the world to keep them from the cannibal life they preferred (Morrison 1987:151).

I am apt to suspect the negroes and in general all the other species of men (for there are four or five different kinds) to be naturally inferior to the whites. There never was a civilized nation of any other complexion than white, or even any individual eminent either in action or speculation. No ingenious manufactures among them, no arts, no sciences. On the other hand, the most rude and barbarous of the whites, such as the ancient Germans, the present Tartars, have still something eminent about them, in their valour, form of government, or some other particular. Such a uniform and constant difference could not happen in so many countries and ages, if nature had not made an original distinction betwixt these breeds of men. Not to mention our colonies, there are Negroe slaves dispersed all over Europe, of which none ever discovered any symptoms of ingenuity, tho' low people, without education, will start up amongst us, and distinguish themselves in every profession. In Jamaica indeed they talk of one negroe as a man of parts and learning; but 'tis likely he is admired for very slender accomplishments like a parrot, who speaks a few words plainly. (David Hume, quoted in Pandian 1985:79).

One swallow does not make a summer, and a few intelligent Negroes do not make a race. . . . To be sure, we should value every man according to his merit—within his own race. It does not follow that virtue would be served by admitting every man or woman that we value, regardless of his race, into those areas of Caucasian social life where mates are chosen (Wesley Critz George, quoted in Ehrlich 1977:10).

On the basis of my theory, I am obviously a believer in the inequality of races. . . . In his fetal development the negro passes through a stage that has already become the final stage for a white man. If retardation contin-ues in the negro, what is still a transitional state may for this race also become a final one. It is possible for all other races to reach the zenith of development now occupied by the white race (L. Bolk, quoted in Ehrlich 1977:10).

The cleanliness of this people, moral and otherwise . . . is a point in itself. By their very exterior you could tell that these were no lovers of water, and, to your distress, you often knew it with your eyes closed. . . .

   All this could scarcely be called very attractive; but it became positively repulsive when, in addition to their physical uncleanliness, you discovered the moral stains on this "chosen people" (Adolf Hitler 1943:57).

What a pity it is that people will go in for racial criticism. The whole thing is perfectly simple. All human beings everywhere are more or less horrible, but they have different fashions of being it, in different places. Consequently, one notices the horribleness of foreigners without noticing one's own—which they notice—just because it is different (White 1947:169).

We may be finding that in some blacks when [the chokehold] is applied, the veins or arteries do not open up as fast as they do in normal people (former Los Angeles Police Chief Daryl F. Gates 1982:A24).

I look at people and I see people (Mamie Mobley, mother of Emmett Till, the fourteen-year-old boy murdered in Mississippi in 1955 for whistling when asked about his reaction to a white woman; quoted in Terkel 1992:21).

America must be kept American. Biological laws show . . . that Nordics deteriorate when mixed with other races (Vice-President Calvin Coolidge, quoted in Kevles 1985).

I think you become an adult when you reach a point where you don't need anyone underneath you. When you can look at theoretical grounds for banishing distinction in the classroom. In the United States the evidence for inferior learning capacity is as inarguable as superior performance on the baseball diamond; yet the question of intelligence remains distinctly unsettled (Ardrey 1970:63).

The American is realistic, concise, exact, irreverent, competent, prompt, and dependable; the Puerto Rican tends to by romantic, diffuse, vague, superstitious, inefficient, dilatory, and unreliable. Where the American is modern, the Puerto Rican is medieval; where the American is scientific, the Puerto Rican is mystical; where the American is accurate, the Puerto Rican is poetic. . . . The Americans are interested in results, the Puerto Ricans are interested in poetry; the American wants facts, the Puerto Rican prefers oratory; the American reads, the Puerto Rican talks (Edward B. Rueter, quoted in Preiswerk & Perrot 1978:51).

The fact that a reasonable hypothesis has not been rigorously proved does not mean that it should be summarily dismissed. It only means that we need more appropriate research for putting it to the test. I believe such definitive research is possible but has not yet been done. So all we are left with are various lines of evidence, no one of which is definitive alone, but which, viewed altogether, make it a not unreasonable hypothesis that genetic factors are strongly implicated in the average Negro–white intelligence difference (Jensen 1972:163).

I am satisfied the present Chinese labor invasion (It is not in any proper sense immigration. Women and children do not come) is pernicious and should be discouraged. Our experience in dealing with the weaker races—the Negroes and the Indians, for example—is not encouraging. We shall oppress the Chinaman, and their presence will make hoodlums or vagabonds of their oppressors. I therefore would consider with favor suitable measures to discourage the Chinese from coming to our shores (President Rutherford B. Hayes, quoted in Sinkler 1972:229).

2. Rewrite the following examples in a nonsexist way:

> Each scientist uses many ways to find out the things that he wants to know. . . . When a scientist experiments, he thinks in a special way. . . . He reads to find out about other experiences. . . . The scientist plans his work step by step. He asks many questions. He decides what he wants to know. Then he does the experiment (*School Library Journal*, September 1987:117).

> Ethnology—or anthropology, to use the more current term—takes man as its object of study but differs from the other sciences of man in striving to understand that object in its most diverse manifestations (Lévi-Strauss, 1985:25).

> I repeat that in individuals a somewhat close relation between mental reaction and bodily build may be found, which is all but absent in populations. Under these circumstances it is necessary to base the investigation of the mental life of man upon a study of the history of cultural forms and of the interrelations between individual mental life and culture (Boas 1940:250).

> Culture or civilization, taken in its wide ethnographic sense, is that complex whole which includes knowledge, belief, art, morals, law, custom, and any other capabilities and habits acquired by man as a member of society (Tylor 1958 [1871]).

References Cited

Alland, Jr., Alexander 1967 *Evolution and Human Behavior*. New York: Natural History Press.

——— 1985 *Human Nature: Darwin's View*. New York: Columbia University Press.

Allport, Gordon W. 1958 [1954] *The Nature of Prejudice*. Garden City, NY: Doubleday Anchor.

Andersen, Margaret L., and Patricia Hill Collins, eds. 1992 *Race, Class, and Gender: An Anthology*. Belmont, CA: Wadsworth.

Appiah, Kwame Anthony 1992 *In My Father's House: Africa in the Philosophy of Culture*. New York: Oxford University Press.

Ardrey, Robert 1970 *The Social Contract: Personal Inquiry into the Evolutionary Sources of Order and Disorder*. New York: Athenaeum Publishers.

Baker, Liva 1991 *The Justice From Beacon Hill: The Life and Times of Oliver Wendell Holmes*. New York: Harper-Collins.

Banton, Michael 1987 *Racial Theories*. Cambridge: Cambridge University Press.

——— 1988 *Racial Consciousness*. Essex, England: Longman.

Banton, Michael, and Jonathan Harwood 1975 *The Race Concept*. New York: Praeger.

Barker, Ernest 1948 *The Politics of Aristotle*. Oxford: Clarendon Press.

Barley, Nigel 1983 *The Innocent Anthropologist: Notes from a Mud Hut*. London: British Museum Publications.

Barlow, Nora, ed. 1958 *The Autobiography of Charles Darwin 1809–1882*. New York: W. W. Norton.

Barrett, Paul H., and Howard E. Gruber 1980 *Metaphysics, Materialism and the Evolution of Mind: Early Writings of Charles Darwin*. Chicago: University of Chicago Press.

Barrett, Stanley R. 1984 *The Rebirth of Anthropological Theory*. Toronto: University of Toronto.

Barzun, Jacques 1958 [1941] *Darwin, Marx, Wagner: Critique of a Heritage.* Garden City, NY: Anchor Books.

———— 1965 *Race: A Study in Superstition.* New York: Harper & Row.

Bates, Daniel G., and Fred Plog 1990 *Cultural Anthropology.* 3rd edition. New York: McGraw-Hill.

Baxter, Paul, and Basil Sansom, eds. 1972 *Race and Social Difference.* Middlesex, England: Penguin Books.

Bell, Derrick 1992 *Faces at the Bottom of the Well: The Permanence of Racism in America.* New York: Basic Books.

Birdsell, J. B. 1975 *Human Evolution.* 2nd edition. Chicago: Rand McNally.

Blauner, Robert 1972 *Racial Oppression in America.* New York: Harper & Row.

———— 1989 *Black Lives, White Lives: Three Decades of Race Relations in America.* Berkeley: University of California Press.

Bleibtreu, Hermann K., and John Meaney 1973 "Race and Racism." In *To See Ourselves: Anthropology and Modern Social Issues.* Thos. Weaver, ed. Pp. 184–188. Glenview, IL: Scott, Foresman.

Boas, Franz 1887 "A Year Among the Eskimo." *Bulletin of the American Geographical Society* 19:383–402. Reprinted in *A Franz Boas Reader: The Shaping of American Anthropology 1883–1911* (1974). George W. Stocking Jr., ed. Pp. 44–55. Chicago: University of Chicago Press.

———— 1908 Letter to Professor J. W. Jenks, 23 Mar. Reprinted in *A Franz Boas Reader: The Shaping of American Anthropology 1883–1911* (1974). George W. Stocking Jr., ed. Pp. 202–205. Chicago: University of Chicago Press.

———— 1909 Letter to Professor J. W. Jenks, 31 Dec. Reprinted in *A Franz Boas Reader: The Shaping of American Anthropology 1883–1911.* (1974). George W. Stocking Jr., ed. Pp. 212–214. Chicago: University of Chicago Press.

———— 1916 "Eugenics." *The Scientific Monthly* 3(5):471–478.

———— 1940 *Race, Language and Culture.* New York: The Free Press.

———— 1969 *Race and Democratic Society.* New York: Biblo and Tannen. (Collection supervised in part by Franz Boas and completed by Ernst Boas.)

Boon, James 1982 *Other Tribes, Other Scribes: Symbolic Anthropology in the Comparative Study of Cultures, Histories, Religions and Texts.* Cambridge: Cambridge University Press.

Bowlby, John 1990 *Charles Darwin: A New Life.* New York: W. W. Norton.

Bowler, Peter J. 1988 *The Non-Darwinian Revolution: Reinterpreting a Historical Myth.* Baltimore, MD: Johns Hopkins University Press.

Boyd, William C. 1950 *Genetics and the Races of Man.* Boston: Little, Brown.

———— 1963 "Genetics and the Human Race." *Science* 140:1057–1065.

Brace, C. Loring 1964a "The Concept of Race." *Current Anthropology* 5:313–320.

———— 1964b "A Non-Racial Approach Toward the Understanding of Human Diversity." In *The Concept of Race.* Ashley Montagu, ed. Pp. 103–152. London: Collier Books.

———— 1991 *The Stages of Human Evolution.* 4th edition. Englewood Cliffs, NJ: Prentice-Hall.

Brace, C. Loring, and Frank B. Livingstone 1971 "On Creeping Jensenism." In *Race and Intelligence.* C. L. Brace, G. R. Gamble, and J. T. Bond, eds. Pp. 64–75. Reprinted in *Race and IQ* (1975). Ashley Montagu, ed. Pp. 151–173. London: Oxford University Press.

Brackman, Arnold C. 1980 *A Delicate Arrangement: The Strange Case of Charles Darwin and Alfred Russel Wallace.* New York: Times Books.

Brodie, Fawn 1974 *Thomas Jefferson: An Intimate History.* New York: W. W. Norton.

Brooks, John Langdon 1984 *Just Before the Origin: Alfred Russel Wallace's Theory of Evolution.* New York: Columbia University Press.

Brown, Michael H. 1990 *The Search for Eve*. New York: Harper & Row.

Brues, Alice M. 1977 *People and Races*. New York: Macmillan.

—— 1991 *The Objective View of Race*. Paper presented at symposium, "Recent Reflections on the Concept of Race," American Anthropological Association Meetings, Chicago, IL. Mimeo.

—— 1992 *Race and How to Teach It*. Mimeo.

Cambridge, Alrick X., and Stephan Feuchtwang 1990 *Antiracist Strategies*. Aldershot, England: Gower.

Campbell, Bernard G. 1992 *Humankind Emerging*. 6th edition. New York: HarperCollins.

Carter, Richard G. 1991 "Hollywood Knows Only One Shade of Black." *New York Times*, 6 April. Pp. 15,21.

Chase, Allan 1980 *The Legacy of Malthus: The Social Costs of the New Scientific Racism*. Urbana: University of Illinois Press.

Churcher, C. S. 1978 "Giraffidae." In *Evolution of African Mammals*. V. J. Maglio and H. B. S. Cooke, eds. Pp. 509–535. Cambridge: Harvard University Press.

Clifford, James 1988 *The Predicament of Culture: Twentieth-Century Ethnography, Literature, and Art*. Cambridge: Harvard University Press.

Coe, Michael D. 1992 *Breaking the Maya Code*. London: Thames and Hudson.

Cole, Douglas 1983 "The Value of a Person Lies in His *Herzenbildung*: Franz Boas' Baffin Island Letter-Diary, 1883–1884." In *Observers Observed: Essays on Ethnographic Fieldwork*. George W. Stocking, Jr., ed. Pp. 13–52. Madison: University of Wisconsin Press.

Collins, Margaret S., Irving W. Wainer, and Theodore A. Bremner 1981 *Science and the Question of Human Equality*. Boulder, CO: Westview Press.

Coon, Carleton S., Stanley M. Garn, and Joseph B. Birdsell 1950 *Races: A Study of the Problems of Race Formation in Man*. Springfield, IL: C C Thomas.

Count, Earl W., ed. 1950 *This Is Race: An Anthology Selected from the International Literature on the Races of Man*. New York: Henry Schuman.

Crapo, Richley H. 1987 *Cultural Anthropology: Understanding Ourselves and Others*. 1st edition. Guilford, CT: Dushkin.

—— 1990 *Cultural Anthropology: Understanding Ourselves and Others*. 2nd edition. Guilford, CT: Dushkin.

Curtin, Philip D. 1964 *The Image of Africa*. Madison: University of Wisconsin Press.

Curtis, L. P., Jr. 1968 *Anglo-Saxons and Celts: A Study of Anti-Irish Prejudice in Victorian England*. Bridgeport, CT: Conference on British Studies at the University of Bridgeport.

Curtis, Lynn 1975 *Violence, Race and Culture*. Lexington, MA: D. C. Heath.

Darlington, C. D. 1969 *The Evolution of Man and Society*. New York: Simon & Schuster.

Darwin, Charles 1898 [1871] *The Descent of Man and Selection in Relation to Sex*. 2nd edition. New York: D. Appleton.

—— 1962 [1860] *The Voyage of the Beagle*. Garden City, NY: Anchor Books.

Darwin, Francis, ed. 1898 *The Life and Letters of Charles Darwin*. 2 vols. New York: D. Appleton.

Dawson, C., and A. S. Woodward 1913 "On the Discovery of a Paleolithic Human Skull and Mandible in a Flint-Bearing Gravel Overlying the Wealden (Hastings Beds) at Piltdown, Fletching (Sussex)." *Quarterly Journal of the Geological Society London* 69:117–151.

Degler, Carl N. 1991 *In Search of Human Nature: The Decline and Revival of Darwinism in American Social Thought*. New York: Oxford University Press.

Demosthenes, Suzie 1991 "Multi-Cultural Diversity Discussions Provide No Solution to Racism on Campus." *The Signal* (Trenton State College Student Newspaper). 29 October, p. 9.

Desmond, Adrian, and James Moore 1992 *Darwin*. New York: Warner Books.

Donald, James, and Ali Rattansi, eds. 1992 *"Race," Culture and Difference.* London: Sage.

Douglas, Mary 1966 *Purity and Danger: An Analysis of Concepts of Pollution and Taboo.* Harmondsworth, England: Penguin Books.

D'Souza, Dinesh 1991 *Illiberal Education: The Politics of Race and Sex on Campus.* New York: Free Press.

Durant, John R. 1979 "Scientific Naturalism and Social Reform in the Thought of Alfred Russel Wallace." *British Journal for the History of Science* 12:33–35.

Edsall, Thomas Byrne, and Mary D. Edsall 1991 *Chain Reaction: The Impact of Race, Rights, and Taxes on American Politics.* New York: W. W. Norton.

Ehrlich, Paul R., and S. Shirley Feldman 1977 [1969] *The Race Bomb: Skin Color, Prejudice, and Intelligence.* New York: Quadrangle.

Eiseley, Loren 1961 *Darwin's Century: Evolution and the Men Who Discovered It.* Garden City, NY: Anchor Books.

—— 1979 *Darwin and the Mysterious Mr. X.* New York: E. P. Dutton.

Eldredge, Niles, and Ian Tattersall 1982 *The Myths of Human Evolution.* New York: Columbia University Press.

Encyclopedia Britannica 1943 Chicago: William Benton.

Feagin, Joe R. 1993 *Racial and Ethnic Relations.* 4th edition. Englewood Cliffs, NJ: Prentice-Hall.

Feagin, Joe R., and Clairece Booher Feagin 1978 *Discrimination American Style: Institutional Racism and Sexism.* Englewood Cliffs, NJ: Prentice-Hall.

Fernandez, Renate Lellep 1990 *A Simple Matter of Salt: An Ethnography of Nutritional Deficiency in Spain.* Berkeley: University of California Press.

Ferraro, Gary 1992 *Cultural Anthropology: An Applied Perspective.* St. Paul, MN: West.

Fichman, Martin 1981 *Alfred Russel Wallace.* Boston: Twayne.

Finkelstein, Norman G. 1992 "How We Inspired Nazis." Letter to Editor, *New York Times.* 18 September, Op-ed page.

Fleming, Robert 1980 "Eugenic Sterilization: Great for What Ails the Poor." *Encore American & Worldwide News* 9:17–19.

Fried, Morton H. 1968 "The Need to End the Pseudoscientific Investigation of Race." In *Science and the Concept of Race.* Margaret Mead, Theodosius Dobzhansky, Ethel Tobach, and Robert E. Light, eds. Pp. 122–131. New York: Columbia University Press.

—— 1978 "Race: A Four Letter Word That Hurts." In *Readings in Physical Anthropology and Archaeology.* David E. K. Hunter and Phillip Whitten, eds. Pp. 312–315. New York: Harper & Row.

Garn, Stanley M. 1971 [1965] *Human Races.* Springfield, IL: C C Thomas.

Gates, Daryl F. [former chief of Los Angeles police] 1982 quoted in *New York Times,* May 12.

Geismar, Maxwell, ed. 1973 *Mark Twain & the Three R's: Race, Religion, Revolution and Related Matters.* Indianapolis, IN: Bobbs-Merrill.

George, Wilma 1964 *Biologist Philosopher: A Study of the Life and Writings of Alfred Russel Wallace.* London: Abelard-Schuman.

Geraads, Denis 1986 *Remarques sur la Systématique et la Phylogénie des Giraffidae.* Geobios 19(4):465–477.

Gillie, Oliver 1977 "Did Sir Cyril Burt Fake His Research on Heritability of Intelligence?" Part I. *Phi Delta Kappan.* February, Pp. 469–471, 492.

Glick, Thomas F., ed. 1980 *The Comparative Reception of Darwinism.* Austin: University of Texas Press.

Gossett, Thomas F. 1963 *Race: The History of an Idea in America.* Dallas: Southern Methodist University Press.

Gould, Stephen Jay 1977 *Ever Since Darwin.* New York: W. W. Norton.

—— 1979 "Perceptive Bees, Birds, and Bacteria." *Natural History* 88(9):25–30.

—— 1980a "Hen's Teeth & Horse's Toes." *Natural History* 89(7): 24–28.

—— 1980b "Natural Selection and the Human Brain: Darwin vs. Wallace." In *The Panda's Thumb.* Pp. 47–59. New York: W. W. Norton.

—— 1980c "Wallace's Fatal Flaw." *Natural History* 89(1):26–40.

—— 1981 *The Mismeasure of Man.* New York: W. W. Norton.

—— 1989 *Wonderful Life: The Burgess Shale and the Nature of History.* New York: W. W. Norton.

—— 1992a "Eve and Her Tree." *Discover* 13:32–34.

—— 1992b "What Is a Species?" *Discover* 13:40–44.

Grant, Madison 1970 [1918] *The Passing of the Great Race, or the Racial Basis of European History.* Salem, NH: Ayer.

Gruber, Howard E. 1981 *Darwin on Man: A Psychological Study of Scientific Creativity.* 2nd edition. Chicago: University of Chicago Press.

Grzimek, Bernhard, ed. 1972–74 "Giraffes." *Animal Life Encyclopedia.* New York: Van Nostrand.

Gumplowicz, Ludwig 1875 *Rasse und Staat: Eine untersuchung uber das gesetz der staatenbildung.* Vienna: verlag der Manzschen Buchhandlung.

Hacker, Andrew 1992 *Two Nations: Black and White, Separate, Hostile, Unequal.* New York: Charles Scribner's.

Handlin, Oscar 1951 *The Uprooted: The Epic Story of the Great Migrations That Made the American People.* Boston: Little, Brown.

—— 1954 *The American People in the Twentieth Century.* Cambridge: Harvard University Press.

Harris, Marvin 1991 *Cultural Anthropology.* 3rd edition. New York: HarperCollins.

Higham, John 1981 *Strangers in the Land: Patterns of American Nativism 1860–1925.* New York: Atheneum.

Himmelfarb, Gertrude 1959 *Darwin and the Darwinian Revolution.* London: Chatto and Windus.

Hitler, Adolf 1943 [1927] *Mein Kampf.* Boston: Houghton Mifflin.

Hodgen, Margaret T. 1964 *Early Anthropology in the Sixteenth and Seventeenth Centuries.* Philadelphia: University of Pennsylvania Press.

Hofstadter, Richard 1955 [1944] *Social Darwinism in American Thought.* Boston: Beacon Press.

Hooks, Bell (aka Gloria Watkins) 1992 *Black Looks: Race and Representation.* Boston: South End Press.

Hooton, Earnest A., and C. Wesley Dupertuis 1955 *The Physical Anthropology of Ireland.* Cambridge, MA: Papers of the Peabody Museum of Archaeology and Ethnology, Vol. XXX, Nos. 1–2.

Howard, Michael C. 1989 *Contemporary Cultural Anthropology.* 3rd edition. Glenview, IL: Scott, Foresman.

Hunter, David E., and Phillip Whitten 1976 *Encyclopedia of Anthropology.* New York: Harper & Row.

Jensen, Arthur R. 1972 *Genetics and Education.* New York: Harper & Row.

Jordan, Winthrop D. 1968 *White over Black: American Attitudes Toward the Negro, 1550–1812.* New York: W. W. Norton.

Kamin, Leon 1974 *The Science and Politics of IQ.* Potomac, MD: Lawrence Erlbaum.

Kaplan, Abraham 1964 *The Conduct of Inquiry: Methodology for Behavioral Science.* San Francisco: Chandler.

Kennedy, J. 1991 Powers vs. Ohio. *The United States Law Week* 59: 4268–4273.

Kevles, Daniel J. 1985 *In the Name of Eugenics: Genetics and the Uses of Human Heredity.* New York: Alfred A. Knopf.

Kohn, David, ed. 1985 *The Darwinian Heritage.* Princeton: Princeton University Press.

Kottler, Malcolm J. 1974 "Alfred Russel Wallace, the Origin of Man, and Spiritualism." *Isis* 65:174–180.

Kozol, Jonathan 1991 *Savage Inequalities*. New York: HarperPerennial.

Kristeva, Julia 1993 *Nations Without Nationalism*. New York: Columbia University Press.

Kroeber, A. L., and Clyde Kluckhohn 1952 *Culture: A Critical Review of Concepts and Definitions*. New York: Random House. (Originally published as Vol. XLVII, No. 1 of the Papers of the Peabody Museum of American Archaeology and Ethnology, Harvard University.)

Kuper, Leo, ed. 1975 *Race, Science and Society*. Paris: UNESCO Press and New York: Columbia University Press.

Lankester, E. Ray 1901 "On Okapia, a New Genus of *Giraffidae*, from Central Africa." *Trans. Zool. Soc. London* 16(1):279–314.

Lebow, Richard Ned 1976 *White Britain and Black Ireland: The Influence of Stereotypes on Colonial Policy*. Philadelphia: Institute for the Study of Human Issues.

Lessing, Doris 1987 *Prisons We Choose to Live Inside*. New York: Harper & Row.

Lévi-Strauss, Claude 1971 "Race and Culture." *International Social Science Journal* 23(4):608–625.

——— 1976 "Race and History." In *Structural Anthropology* 2:323–362. Chicago: University of Chicago Press.

——— 1985 *The View from Afar*. New York: Basic Books.

Lewin, Roger 1989 *Human Evolution: An Illustrated Introduction*. 2nd edition. Boston: Blackwell Scientific.

Lewis, C. S. 1952 *The Voyage of the Dawn Treader*. New York: Collier Books.

Lewontin, R. C. 1978 "The Fallacy of Biological Determinism." In *Readings in Physical Anthropology and Archaeology*. David E. Hunter and Phillip Whitten, eds. Pp. 319–323. New York: Harper & Row.

Lichter, S. Robert, Linda S. Lichter, and Stanley Rothman 1991 *Watching America: What Television Tells Us About Our Lives*. New York: Prentice-Hall.

Linnaeus, Carolus 1758 [1736] *Systema Naturae*. Leyden, Holland.

Littlefield, A., L. Lieberman, and L. Reynolds 1982 "Redefining Race: The Potential Demise of a Concept in Physical Anthropology." *Current Anthropology* 23(96):641–655.

Livingstone, Frank B. 1962 "On the Nonexistence of Human Races." *Current Anthropology* 3:279–281. Reprinted with revisions in *The Concept of Race* (1964). Ashley Montagu, ed. Pp. 46–60. New York: Collier Books.

——— 1964 "Human Populations." In *Horizons of Anthropology* (1964). Sol Tax, ed. Chicago: Aldine Publishing Company. Reprinted in *Man in Evolutionary Perspective* (1973). C. Loring Brace and James Metress, eds. Pp. 3–9. New York: John Wiley.

Loehlin, John C., Gardner Lindzey, and J. N. Spuhler 1975 *Race Differences in Intelligence*. San Francisco: W. H. Freeman.

Malefijt, Annemarie DeWaal 1974 *Images of Man: A History of Anthropological Thought*. New York: Alfred A. Knopf.

Mandeville, Sir John. See M. C. Seymour

Marchant, James 1975 (1916) *Alfred Russel Wallace: Letters and Reminiscences*. New York: Arno Press.

Marcus, George, and Michael Fischer 1986 *Anthropology as Cultural Critique: An Experimental Moment in the Human Sciences*. Chicago: University of Chicago Press.

Marger, Martin N. 1994 [1985] *Race and Ethnic Relations: American and Global Perspectives*. Belmont, CA: Wadsworth.

Marks, Richard Lee 1991 *Three Men of the Beagle*. New York: Alfred A. Knopf.

Marshall, Gloria A. 1968 "Racial Classifications: Popular and Scientific." In *Science and the Concept of Race*. Margaret Mead, Theodosius Dobzhansky, Ethel Tobach, and Robert E. Light, eds. Pp. 149–164. New York: Columbia University Press.

McKinney, H. Lewis 1972 *Wallace and Natural Selection*. New Haven: Yale University Press.

Mead, Margaret, Theodosius Dobzhansky, Ethel Tobach, and Robert E. Light, eds. 1968 *Science and the Concept of Race*. New York: Columbia University Press.

Milner, Richard 1990 *The Encyclopedia of Evolution: Humanity's Search for Its Origins*. New York: Facts on File.

Molnar, Stephen 1992 *Human Variation: Races, Types and Ethnic Groups*. 3rd edition. Englewood Cliffs, NJ: Prentice-Hall.

Montagu, Ashley 1964 [1942] *Man's Most Dangerous Myth: The Fallacy of Race*. 4th edition. Cleveland: World.

———— ed. 1969 *The Concept of Race*. London: Collier Books.

———— ed. 1975 *Race and IQ*. London: Oxford University Press.

———— 1977 "Race: The History of the Concept." In *Human Evolution*. C. Loring Brace and M. F. Ashley Montagu, eds. Pp. 366–386. New York: Macmillan.

Morgan, Edmund S. 1972 "Slavery and Freedom: The American Paradox." *The Journal of American History* LIX(1):5–29.

Morrison, Toni 1987 *Beloved*. New York: Alfred A. Knopf.

Ms. Magazine 1992 "Indigenous Peoples— 1492 and 1992." III(2):20–21, 88.

Nelson, Harry D., and Robert Jurmain 1991 *Introduction to Physical Anthropology*. 5th edition. St. Paul, MN: West.

Oberg, Kalervo 1954 *Culture Shock*. Address presented to the Women's Club of Rio de Janeiro, Brazil. Reprint No. A-239. Indianapolis, IN: Bobbs-Merrill.

———— 1960 "Culture Shock: Adjustment to New Environments." *Practical Anthropology* 7:177–182.

Osborn, Henry Fairfield 1928 *Impressions of Great Naturalists*. 2nd edition. New York: Charles Scribner's.

Pandian, Jacob 1985 *Anthropology and the Western Tradition: Toward an Authentic Anthropology*. Prospect Heights, IL: Waveland.

Patterson, H. E. H. 1985 "The Recognition Concept of Species." In *Species and Speciation*. Pp. 21–39. Pretoria, South Africa: Transvaal Museum (Transvaal Museum Monograph No. 4).

Patterson, Orlando 1991 *Freedom, Freedom in the Making of Western Culture*. Vol. 1. New York: Basic Books.

Peters, William 1971 *A Class Divided*. Garden City, NY: Doubleday.

Pettigrew, Thomas F. 1971 *Racially Separate or Together?* New York: McGraw-Hill.

Piel, Gerard 1978 "IQ: Failing the Test." *The Sciences* 18(1):7–9, 23.

Preiswerk, Roy, and Dominique Perrot 1978 *Ethnocentrism and History: Africa, Asia and Indian America in Western Textbooks*. New York: Nok.

Rauschning, Hermann 1940 *The Voice of Destruction*. New York: G. P. Putnam's.

Relethford, John 1990 *The Human Species: An Introduction to Biological Anthropology*. Mountain View, CA: Mayfield.

Ridley, Mark 1993 *Evolution*. Boston: Blackwell Scientific.

Ripley, William Z. 1899 *The Races of Europe*. New York: Appleton-Century.

Rodriguez, Clara E. 1989 *Puerto Ricans: Born in the U.S.A.* Winchester, MA: Unwin Hyman.

Rose, Peter I. 1974 *They and We: Racial and Ethnic Relations in the United States*. 2nd edition. New York: Random House.

Russell, Bertrand 1945 *A History of Western Philosophy*. New York: Simon & Schuster.

Saveth, Edward Norman 1948 *American Historians and European Immigrants 1875–1925*. New York: Columbia University Press.

Schaefer, Richard T. 1990 *Racial and Ethnic Groups*. 4th edition. New York: HarperCollins.

—— 1992 *Sociology*. 4th edition. New York: McGraw-Hill.

Schultz, Emily A., and Robert H. Lavenda 1987 *Cultural Anthropology: A Perspective on the Human Condition*. St. Paul, MN: West.

Segal, Daniel A. 1991 "'The European': Allegories of Racial Purity." *Anthropology Today* 7(5):7–9.

Seymour, M. C., ed. 1968 *Mandeville's Travels*. London: Oxford University Press.

Shanklin, Eugenia 1981 "Before Darwin." *Science Digest* 89(8):37.

—— 1990 "The Odyssey of the *Afo-a-Kom*." *African Arts XXIII* (4):62–69; 95–96.

Shanklin, Eugenia, and Larry L. Mai, eds. 1981 "Joseph B. Birdsell: A Conceptual Biography." In *Anthropology UCLA* 7:21–53, *The Perception of Evolution*. Los Angeles: University of California at Los Angeles Press.

Shreeve, James 1990 "Argument over a Woman." *Discover* 11(8):52–59.

Simpson, George E., and J. Milton Yinger 1953 *Racial and Cultural Minorities: An Analysis of Prejudice and Discrimination*. New York: Harper & Row.

Singer, Ronald, and Edouard L. Boné 1960 "Modern Giraffes and the Fossil Giraffids of Africa." *Annals of the South African Museum* XLV(4):375–603.

Sinkler, George 1972 *The Racial Attitudes of American Presidents from Abraham Lincoln to Theodore Roosevelt*. Garden City, NY: Anchor Books.

Solomon, Barbara Miller 1956 *Ancestors and Immigrants: A Changing New England Tradition*. Cambridge: Harvard University Press.

Sowell, Thomas 1990 *Preferential Policies: An International Perspective*. New York: William Morrow.

Spencer, Frank 1990a *The Piltdown Papers*. London: Oxford University Press.

—— 1990b *Piltdown: A Scientific Forgery*. London: Oxford University Press.

Stanton, William 1960 *The Leopard's Spots*. Chicago: University of Chicago Press.

Staski, Edward, and Jonathan Marks 1992 *Evolutionary Anthropology*. Fort Worth: Harcourt Brace Jovanovich.

Stefan, Susan 1989 "Whose Egg Is It Anyway?: Reproductive Rights of Incarcerated, Institutionalized and Incompetent Women." *Nova Law Review* 13:405–456.

Stepan, Nancy 1982 *The Idea of Race in Science: Great Britain 1800–1960*. Hamden, CT: Archon Books.

Stocking, Jr., George W. 1968 *Race, Culture, and Evolution: Essays in the History of Anthropology*. New York: Free Press.

—— ed. 1974 *A Franz Boas Reader: The Shaping of American Anthropology 1883–1911*. Chicago: University of Chicago Press.

Tambiah, Stanley 1989 "Ethnic Conflict in the World Today." *American Ethnologist* 16(2):335–349.

Terkel, Studs 1992 *Race: How Blacks and Whites Think and Feel About the American Obsession*. New York: New Press.

Thorne, Alan G., and Milford H. Wolpoff 1992 "The Multiregional Evolution of Humans." *Scientific American* 266:76–83.

Tianyuan, Li, and Dennis A. Etler 1992 "New Middle Pleistocene Hominid Crania from Yunxian in China." *Nature* 357(6377):404–407.

Tierney, John, Lynda Wright, and Karen Springen 1988 "The Search for Adam and Eve." *Newsweek* 11 January, Pp. 46–52.

Tobias, Phillip V. 1972 [1961] "The Meaning of Race." Reprinted in *Race and Social Difference*. Paul Baxter and Basil Sansom, eds. Middlesex, England: Penguin. Pp. 19–43.

Twain, Mark. See Maxwell Geismar, ed.

Tylor, E. B. 1958 [1871] *Primitive Culture*. 2 vol. New York: Harper Torch Books.

Van den Berghe, Pierre 1967 *Race and Racism*. New York: John Wiley.

—— 1970 *Race and Ethnicity: Essays in Comparative Sociology.* New York: Basic Books.

Van Maanen, John 1988 *Tales of the Field: On Writing Ethnography.* Chicago: University of Chicago Press.

Wade, Nicholas 1978 "Voice from the Dead Names New Suspect for Piltdown Hoax." *Science* 202:1062.

Wallace, A. R. 1875 *On Miracles and Modern Spiritualism: Three Essays.* London: James Burns.

Wallace, Alfred Russel 1864 "The Origin of Human Races and the Antiquity of Man Deduced from the Theory of 'Natural Selection.'" *Journal of the Anthropological Society* 2:clviii–clxx.

—— 1905 *My Life: A Record of Events and Opinions.* 2 vols. London: Chapman & Hall.

—— 1913 *Social Environment and Moral Progress.* New York: Cassell.

—— 1969 [1853] *A Narrative of Travels on the Amazon and Rio Negro, with an Account of the Native Tribes.* New York: Haskell House.

Weiner, J. S. 1981 [1955] *The Piltdown Forgery.* New York: Dover.

Weiss, Mark L., and Alan E. Mann 1978 *Human Biology and Behavior.* Boston: Little, Brown.

Wellman, David T. 1977 *Portraits of White Racism.* Cambridge: Cambridge University Press.

West, Cornel, 1993 *Race Matters.* Boston: Beacon Press.

White, T. H. 1989 [1947] *The Elephant and the Kangaroo.* New York: Signet Books New American Library, Penguin Books.

Williams, Patricia J. 1991 *The Alchemy of Race and Rights.* Cambridge: Harvard University Press.

Wilson, Allan C. 1990 *The Search for Mitochondrial Eve.* Talk given at Rutgers University/Leakey Foundation dinner, 20 October, New Brunswick, NJ.

Wilson, Allan C., and Rebecca L. Cann 1992 "The Recent African Genesis of Humans." *Scientific American* 266:68–73.

Winslow, J. H., and A. Meyer 1983 "The Perpetrator at Piltdown." *Science* 83(4):32–43.

Wolker, Robert 1977 "The Analogies of Nature." *Times Literary Supplement* 11 March, p. 262.

Yamato, Gloria 1988 "Something About the Subject Makes It Hard to Name." In *Changing Our Power: An Introduction to Women's Studies.* Jo Whitehorse Cochran, Donna Langston, and Carolyn Woodward, eds. Pp. 3–6. Dubuque, IA: Kendall-Hunt.

Zuckerman, Lord S. 1990 "A Phony Ancestor." Review of *Piltdown: A Scientific Forgery,* and *The Piltdown Papers, 1908–1955: The Correspondence and Other Documents Relating to the Piltdown Forgery,* by Frank Spencer. *New York Review of Books.* 37 (8 November): 12–16.

Index